Vittoria Pasquini
THE LEGEND OF BUSBY
Translated by **Gino Moliterno**

Introduction by **Filippo La Porta**

Riverton Press

Vittoria Pasquini

The Legend of Busby

Translated from Italian by Gino Moliterno

Introduction by Filippo La Porta

Cover: Original image by Elena Palombi Luff

With collage additions by Simona Gasco and colour adjustments by Raffaella Ottaviani

Book Design: Leonie Lane

ISBN:

9780645033533 paperback

9780645033588 e-book

First published by Riverton Press, Sydney, Australia, 2024

© Copyright Vittoria Pasquini 2024

The publisher acknowledges permission to quote from *Oleander, Jacaranda: A Childhood Perceived*, by Penelope Lively, published by David Higham Associates, UK, 1994.

For Martina, Elena, Emer, and Valerio, always

Your house is your larger body.
It grows in the sun and sleeps in the stillness of the night; and it is not dreamless.
Does not your house dream? and dreaming, leave the city for a grove or hill-top?

            Kahil Gibran, *The Prophet*

All habits are geared towards the linear, the sequential,
but memory refuses such orderliness.
  Penelope Lively, *Oleander, Jacaranda: A Childhood Perceived*

INTRODUCTION

"Wayfarer, your footprints are / the path and nothing more; / wayfarer, the path does not exist, / the path is made by walking". Antonio Machado's verses could stand as the seal to this memoir in the form of a novel. The woman who narrates it celebrates taking her leave, after 18 years, from that protective "sandstone castle" that was Busby: *"we understood that life is a journey full of pauses but still a journey, and that now it's time to begin again"*. Busby, an old building a few minutes away from one of Sydney's beaches - redesigned and renovated - has welcomed people from all over the world: defeated and disappointed revolutionaries, world-travellers, exiles, hippies. The concrete utopia of a heterogeneous but supportive micro community, a cosmopolitan space where diversity is fraternally welcomed. A little like Arlo Guthrie's Alice's restaurant in that poignant film by Arthur Penn, where the hippy community, temporarily housed in a deconsecrated church (with the support of the restaurant), is starting to come undone, and its members beginning to re-integrate into society. The first-person narrator, after losing her two husbands, goes there with her children, and there creates new relationships, contemplating the ocean from a large window, rethinking her turbulent biography as a young Catholic, a revolutionary, a feminist, a teacher

of Italian in Australia, learning the stoic-epicurean art of *carpe diem*, mixing yoga and Vipassana meditation. I will say nothing regarding her prior existence, in which she played countless roles with the same conviction, united only (as is recounted here) by the passing of the years. I only refer you to the text itself, which is consistently enjoyable, even at its most dramatic moments. Busby's almost twenty years mark a spiritual journey, something of a "conversion" and a rebirth. Many clues point the way; I limit myself to underlining the importance bestowed on the bathroom and the kitchen in the large house, two places commonly considered secondary (the so-called "conveniences"): "the bathroom is a marvel", "the kitchen is a little jewel". Thich Nhat Hanh recommended meditating while cleaning the house: high and low, heaven and earth, the sublime and the trash a continuous hybridization. She repaints the room pink, a colour that becomes a little cloying especially at sunset, like cotton candy at country village festivals. But life is also made of cotton candy, as well as apparently useless, free things... Her rejection of linear time and every notion of a univocal identity recalls the great Nigerian Yoruba writer, Akomolafe Bayo: *"quantum queerness deconstructs identity and undoes the space-time project that would see us all get home in one piece"*. Rather, *"being at home is a preparation for exile"*. Vittoria Pasquini ideally engages in her own dance of "home and exile", of past and future. The author's most beautiful and original literary invention is the Greek chorus that acts as a counterpoint to the story, the "voices-off": "... that they were gay and didn't fit in well at home, that Australia was less homophobic than their country, that they had come for work and then remained, that they had become enchanted by the natural environment here...". There is a percussive "that" which impresses a rhythm on the entire narrative, like a drum in Dionysian festivals, or in Yoruba ritual ceremonies.

The book you are about to read is, in the style of Alessandro Manzoni, the story of a soul, fatally "twisted" (especially for those born under the sign of Gemini). The story of a soul that is much more real than History and its great events, its wars and revolutions. There is a passage that seems decisive to me. When she talks about the fear of death that she had as a young girl. Then, at a certain point, she overcame it by imagining dying on a barricade, in a red poncho and with a clenched fist. My/our generation - of which this text is a truthful story - demanded of politics more than it could give them: redemption. Yet the only thing by which death could be defeated was not so much courage as much as "the depth of the ocean", the discovery of Reality, within which life and death are no longer separated. It's precisely what happens to Prince Andrei Bolkonskij in *War and Peace*, when, having been wounded at Austerlitz, he contemplates the boundless sky above him, so much greater than human nature and our ephemeral story: "Nothing, nothing exists outside of it. But not even it exists; nothing exists except silence, except stillness". Vittoria Pasquini had to travel 16,300 km –the very distance between the Flaminio district and Sydney – to find stillness and infinity.

Filippo La Porta

The sandstone castle was very old; old that is, for the white Australia of the invaders, but very new for the original inhabitants who, although they had never built a castle, had lived in Australia and therefore also on that hill facing the sea for at least 65,000 years.

That the street was called Busby and that, as a result, everyone called the castle Busby, was because one of the first buyers of land in that area of Sydney had indeed been a certain William Busby.

Even if it was said in the area that the name Busby had to do instead with the fur hat worn by the mounted artillery of the Queen of England and so, in some way or other, bore the signature of two brothers who were the stonemasons who had built the castle at the end of the nineteenth century, the oldest building in that area. Busby was also said to have been built in part with sandstone blocks left over from Bronte House (the most important villa in the area dedicated to the memory of Admiral Nelson, Duke of Bronte), in part with those ripped out of the hill there, where the castle stood, by the two brothers themselves. But this was oral history and no one had any documents to prove the truth of the Busby legend.

Located in the south-eastern part of the Bronte district and high above the sea with a beautiful view of Clovelly Bay and of Coogee Bay further in the distance, the castle was double-storied and had its mirror twin on its right. Originally, on the upper floor at the front, facing north, there must have been a long balcony connecting the two French doors of the large bedroom, always bathed in sunshine in the morning. On the same landing but facing east there was another medium-large room that led via a French door into what had once been a veranda and which, later enclosed, had become the third bedroom. Extended outside the original walls of the castle and therefore without the thickness or freshness of the air typical of a room inside the walls, the third room was built of very friable material, with many small windows aligned on the south side which, however, had a beautiful view of the sea. This long and narrow room could be accessed either from the door connected to the middle room or by clambering up the stairs to a window that once must have directly faced the sea and now instead opened onto the former veranda.

On the ground floor the entrance from the street was through a neglected garden and a door that must have seen better times.

A long and dark corridor opened up immediately on the left to a room full of light with a huge scalloped window, arched at the top, and with two very narrow and long side windows in the same design. A faded painting in the nineteenth century English style dominated on the opposite wall.

In the middle of the corridor, always on the left, was the bathroom with crumbling walls and a bathtub with lion's head feet and then, at the end, the kitchen and a small living room that extended into a fairly large and windowless alcove. The kitchen led out into a microscopic glassed-in veranda with stairs that descended to the three-terraces of the back garden and, below the house, to the cellar/laundry. At the bottom, on the last terrace, two twin garages.

The castle had been variously described by visitors and occasional passers-by as an ancient Tuscan villa, a Yemeni house, the house in Verona of Shakespeare's Juliet, and at times like an Italian Renaissance-era baptistery.

PROLOGUE

A tall, thin man with black hair and a pained face, the woman at his side dishevelled, her eyes lost who knows where, the little boy with a baby bottle and a lion cub soft-toy reduced to a rag, a young girl, silent, and with the look of not wanting to be there.

They enter the castle. They are met by a group of people, obviously their friends, who all appear moved. They're smeared with paint; they must have been painting walls, the smell is in the air.

All eyes are focused on the man who can hardly stand up; the room is ready, someone says.

Two friends offer to accompany him upstairs; the large bright room with the king-size futon welcomes him.

Below, people confabulate in whispers. The woman, with her two children next to her, hurriedly explains; one can tell she has already repeated the same story many times.

A few people, perhaps to distract her, show her the work they've done. The renovations were supposed to be done by an architect and a professional company because the interior had been in very bad shape when the woman and the man, enthusiastically just a few months earlier, had bought Busby at auction. Now there's no money but it no longer matters; the woman looks around with distracted eyes, touched only by the generosity of her friends.

They throw a pasta together. The group is mixed but the Italians prevail in the kitchen. The child is passed from arms to arms, and cuddled. The girl responds in monosyllables and only if questioned.

There is a sense of suspension. No one speaks of anything but the moment, of this long moment of waiting.

The doctor is coming soon; let's see what he says.

THE RETURN

At the sound of the car braking, the castle door opens.

From it emerge the daughter, no longer a girl but now a young woman, and a female friend of the family.

They move towards the car from which the smiling child sporting sunglasses too big for his face scrambles out; he must be, at most, nine years old, the little toy lion, now aged but always loved, clenched to his chest.

The mother greets everyone in an agitated voice; inside the car there are the two kittens which have driven her mad during the entirety of the trip. She asks her daughter to pick them up; the conversations quickly intersect, the tone is cheerful, slightly emotional.

The car is bursting at the seams, the greater part of their belongings will arrive soon with the removalists. Everyone is hungry, a big plate of steaming pasta awaits them in the kitchen.

For the moment the woman and the child will stay in the middle room upstairs; also the two cats that have been locked inside there to let them settle down. Some tenants, friends of hers, will need to leave for the woman to be able to take back the large bedroom, and the child the middle room. Or perhaps she will take the former veranda and the child always the middle room. Or maybe. She doesn't know yet; it will be decided later. Everything is still up in the air. As they are.

In the evening the friend and the daughter go out.

The woman closes herself off in the room with the sleeping boy; the cats are restless because they would like to explore. Suddenly she is gripped by a great melancholy.

The image of Giacomo suffering in the room next door six years earlier, and that first moment without hope that she will always fear might repeat, pass before her eyes, vivid as a high-definition film.

Was it a mistake to leave Canberra, the Australian National University, where she was well off, and that beautiful house in Hovea Street which represented her *Vita Nova*?

Tears flow, the cats meow mercilessly, the child wakes up agitated; luckily she can look after him, hug him, cuddle him until he falls asleep again. The passage of time, she has learned, will help her.

*

Little by little, life begins again for the woman and for the child.

The beach welcomes them warmly every day. From Busby to Bronte

Beach takes eight minutes going downhill in the morning, ten minutes coming back uphill in the afternoon. It's December, the height of summer, and the woman has no need to structure her days which unfold leisurely between dips in the sea and soccer matches. The child practises obstinately and passionately with the ball. The mother acts as his football partner. She still has a powerful kick from years of playing with brothers and cousins. When she can, she walks up and down along the cliff. So many decisions to make; she's undecided as never before.

After a week of being cloistered, Coco and Cosmo hesitantly venture into the garden. Wicked old tom-cat Jerry lies in ambush at any time of day; that is his territory. The two kittens will have to adapt.

The daughter understandably finds it hard to readjust to her mother, to her little brother, to timetables, accustomed as she has been to living very freely for the last five years. Shortly after Christmas she decides to go on a trip with friends to the Simpson Desert. The family friend also leaves for Byron Bay.

The mother takes it badly. She starts painting the former veranda pink; it will be her bedroom. She spends the days at the beach with the child, in the evening she feels alone in the castle; immediately after sunset the scent of honeysuckle momentarily makes her giddy. She likes the English word, honeysuckle, more than the Italian *caprifoglio*.

The small glassed-in veranda behind the kitchen becomes her refuge. It is open to the sea, to the sky, to the garden below. It is there that she works on her thesis for a graduate Diploma in Second Language

Acquisition, in the evenings when the child is asleep and does not notice that she still smokes the odd cigarette.

*

It is early in the morning. February; perhaps eight o'clock; perhaps a Monday.

The castle rings with excited voices; feet rush down the stairs; hurried farewells.

The door opens. The woman and the child rush out across the small garden which now has its grass freshly cut and its fence freshly painted.

The sound of car doors slamming.

The child makes the journey from Busby to Woollahra Primary School full of excitement at the prospect of meeting with little friends; the mother makes it with apprehension for all the things that she has to remind him of, and which he is likely to forget. Kisses and goodbyes; more kisses.

An hour of traffic from there to the Australian Catholic University, her new workplace. The woman spends it listing all the reasons why she regrets leaving the Australian National University and her colleagues there. She remembers the old times fondly, when she coordinated the Italian program, throwing out the textbooks in favour of a more active involvement of students doing presentations in schools, radio programs, conducting interviews with Italians in Canberra, preparing theatrical pieces and television programs with them. Now at the new university she's a cog in a gear that repeatedly turns in the same old way. She keeps hoping that SBS Radio will accept her proposal for an educational program so she can immerse herself in a different, and above all creative work, but at this point she thinks it unlikely.

Almost in a trance she crosses the city in the morning rush hour, negotiating the CBD with its skyscrapers and the bay that bustles all around it. She drives through the inner suburban belt once inhabited by the respectable bourgeoisie that now prefers waterside villas with breathtaking views. After nearly an hour she's finally at Strathfield and the Mount Saint Mary Campus. Amid the metropolitan chaos, nostalgic for the calm and greenery of Canberra, she reflects on how different her life is now: from Lecturer she has reverted to being Assistant Lecturer, on an annual contract instead of a permanent position, with a much smaller salary, a run-down house and the relationship with her daughter – her main reason for returning to Sydney – still complicated.

Late in the afternoon she goes to Bondi to pick up the child from Vera, the Chinese woman who runs a small after-school program at home. She also has a son of the same age as hers, they are in class together.

The woman has sent the child to Vera without knowing much about her because a fortune-teller in Canberra had told her that a certain

"Vera" would help her on her return to Sydney.

The child is not particularly happy with this arrangement, three afternoons a week; he is not even happy to be back in Sydney. He has left behind in Canberra his best friend, Ale, the house with its big beautiful garden and his junior football club which had won the local championship.

Mother and son return to Busby, both feeling rather melancholic.

The castle is illuminated and this heartens the woman; the child is happy to hug his beloved kittens again.

*

Late afternoon, almost evening, candles are burning everywhere in the castle.

The inhabitants are there together in the large room upstairs; there is also an unexpected and very welcome guest.

It's clear that something important is about to happen.

Hushed silence, a drum begins to roll, the air is scented with flowers and incense.

Silence. Several minutes of silence, the drum again, then one moves on to the next room; more incense, more flowers, more candles, more silence.

Slowly, one after another, the kitchen, the bathroom, the storage room under the stairs and the laundry room, are visited, inhabited in silence, breathed in by the group, which has now become a single body.

At the end of the ceremony they are all happy and excited; slightly embarrassed before beginning to speak again, then, little by little, they loosen up.

The woman above all. She was the one who initiated the idea of the *puja*, a purification of the castle. She wants to drive away the suffering that she imagines at night with open eyes, pain that saturates the sandstone walls and timber floors, still trapped, six years later, in the air of both the large and small crannies of this mansion. The place fascinates her but it's still slightly unsettling.

The unexpected guest also has his own account to settle with Busby. He wants to make peace with his grandmother, a former owner of the manor who had died before he could apologise for his many escapades when, an adolescent spending his vacations with her, he did nothing but get drunk and take drugs, thinking that she wouldn't notice. Having by chance met the friend of the family at a party who had invited him to the ceremony, he now feels that, finally, his grandmother has forgiven him.

He is now a painter on his way to Japan where he will exhibit his paintings in Tokyo.

A superb pasta, toasts galore, there is even a dessert to finish with.

*

After some time, an orange tree is planted in the front garden of Busby, in front of the large triple window.

In the back garden, the first level is occupied by the cats who now more effectively defend their bowls always full of food. The other two levels are still in a comatose state; through the doors of the garages one can see old furniture, unopened boxes, a Swedish backrest, golf clubs that have never been used can be glimpsed. Then, one day, a terrifying discovery: many of the spiders are venomous.

The family friend has now installed herself in the large room upstairs, the child is still in the middle room, the daughter in the front room on the ground floor and the woman is in the pink-painted veranda.

The furniture brought from Canberra which was made to fit with great difficulty through the narrow corridor – furniture that, in part had originally come from Italy and in part had been purchased in Canberra – will clearly provide a different tone to the environment. From a student shared-house look, it will graduate to that of fallen nobility or genteel poverty.

There is often a coming and going of old friends and acquaintances, a continual opening and closing of the castle door, a great deal of shouting, music, discussions, altercations, and also laughter, especially in the late evening.

The clatter of dishes, the aroma of tomato sauce.

*

The pink room is now her room. If she were to say why she chose pink, the woman would be embarrassed because pink is a colour that she has always avoided like the plague: too saccharine. The bright red of revolution, the new-age orange-red have always been her favourite colours, but, of course, it's impossible for her to even contemplate going to sleep surrounded by red walls. In addition, she has discovered that the southern light that filters through the windows overlooking the sea verges on blue, and so, after all the trouble of painting the cracked walls pink (is there asbestos? ... she'd rather not investigate) she also suspects that it's the wrong colour. And yet she chose pink on impulse, she remembers it well, even if she doesn't recall why. Perhaps for a change. At times she does unpredictable things to put herself to the test, to see things from a completely different point of view.

At dawn, however, pink is definitely the right colour. The sun rises from the side window above her bed, an old window, difficult to open, and the light at dawn is rosy orange, so the whole room shines in all its glory. But at sunset, on the other wall, the one with the many windows overlooking the sea, the blue light from outside makes the pink of the inside walls cloying; it resembles the colour of artificial candy floss at Italian village fairs.

The long and narrow glass table, a Frate designed by Enzo Mari, which she bought in Canberra from former colleague and fleeting lover, Gianluca, and which she has placed in a prominent position facing the sea, reflects the light of the sky in the afternoon. It is difficult to use in those hours, better in the morning or in the evening.

She bought the table with the money she had won in the Second of June Literary Award sponsored by the Italian Consulate General in Sydney. It's an award that she regards as embarrassing, given that she received it in Australia where she was competing with non-professional Italian writers. Nor is she, of course, but she would have liked to have a verdict on her writings to have come from an Italian jury in Italy. Nevertheless, the money was just right, one thousand dollars, the exact amount the ex-lover was asking for the table.

As for the "Australian Slides", the title she has given to her collection of very short stories, it does still seem to her today that they do express those deep feelings she experienced in her first days in Australia; let's just say she's not ashamed of them.

Now the table that she likes so much seems to remind her, or rather admonish her, that it's time to grab the bull by the horns.

Photography is, at this stage, something that belongs to the past. It's from a time when Giacomo was in her life, full of energy, enthusiasm and even money to be able to spoil her with all the cameras, lenses, and expensive tripods available, as well as also paying for all the developing, proofing and printing. Now, with him gone and with little money, what remains is writing; it costs nothing and has always been a fixation around which she has hovered, dawdled with, but continually postponed by inventing distractions. Underlying it all, she now understands, has been fear.

But of what? Perhaps of the comparison with one brother who is a writer, certain of becoming one from an early age, and the other, a devoted journalist? Perhaps she doesn't want to clash with them; she's the older sister and might want to protect them, not compete with them. But compete in what way? If she hasn't even tried, really tried; she hasn't submitted herself to the necessary discipline, she has never put herself to the test.

Her return to Sydney, so agonising, so racked with indecision, encompasses the writing project together with many others. But in this pink room with this Frate table facing the sea, it is the only project.

*

The middle room upstairs has been inhabited by various friends and acquaintances in succession. It is the least interesting room in the house and has no particularly attractive features. From the fairly small window one can only see the house next door and, if one leans out over its thick sandstone sill, a sliver of sea in the far distance. It is neither big enough nor small enough to be distinctive. It's just a medium-sized room not particularly well-lit. In addition, it connects through what had once been a French window with the former veranda, now become the pink bedroom. And this, obviously, is a disadvantage if the two rooms were to be occupied by complete strangers or, in any case, by people who wanted some privacy.

One advantage, however, the middle room does have. Being a room wholly inside the old walls and with only a small window, it keeps cool in summer and warm in winter.

On their return from Canberra, that room becomes the child's room, immediately and permanently.

The child likes it, he feels protected. And then, there's another great advantage: it's a very quiet room, the walls don't allow noises to come through. If the child closes the door he can indulge himself in his fantasies, above all playing with his Lego, without his beloved cats, or any of the many inhabitants or visitors to the castle, unwittingly stepping on any of his intricate constructions.

Furthermore, at the beginning of their residence in Sydney, the room's easy access to his mother's pink room renders it ideally placed.

In the Canberra winter, the bitter cold, but also the desire to cuddle and to feel the warm body of the child close to her, had prompted the woman – after the departure, one after another, and for various reasons, of temporary or long-term guests – to let the child sleep in her large bed. In addition she still had (and it was difficult to confess it at nearly fifty!) a slight fear of living alone; the child kept her company and she felt able, there in the big bed, to protect him from the possible intrusion of an imaginary, but forever present in her unconscious, nocturnal thief. This was her longstanding fear, perhaps inherited from her mother who had once spoken to her during a summer vacation at Tagliacozzo, of waking up in the night and "perceiving" the presence of a man in her room, possibly a robber. Since then, the agitated and frightened face of her mother had remained imprinted in the woman's memory and, whenever she found herself home alone at night, it would come back into her mind and make her anxious.

Thus, in Canberra, the child had become accustomed to sleeping with his mother but now he's grown and she thinks it's time for him to break away from her and she from him. The house is full of people, she no longer feels alone at night at the mercy of an intruder and she can always get up and go to her son, should he wake, without feeling the cold penetrating her bones. And Sydney has a subtropical climate and winters are never really cold.

One thing that worries her a lot in her relationship with her son is his education. They share an almost symbiotic relationship, but the lack of a male figure in the boy's life forces her to act as a father and a mother.

How is it to be mother and father at the same time? She observes herself at times and finds herself alternating between positions that she considers rational, decisive, without a second thought, with decidedly more transactional attitudes governed by affection and the desire to see the child happy, often to the point of indulgence.

The aggravating factor for her is that she not only has a son, but also a daughter, without a father; two different fathers and both absent but for different reasons. Silvio, the father of the daughter is far away, in Rome, or travelling in the East, therefore he's almost non-existent, except for the visits that his daughter makes to see him once a year in Italy at Christmas. Or for the father's sporadic trips to Australia and the letters they exchange which seem to the woman to be ever more distant from the challenges that her daughter, first as a teenager and now as a young woman, needs to face. But the daughter has now grown, with so many mistakes made in her upbringing by both mother and father. The woman admits this with regret but she is aware that now, more and more, she can only engage in a relationship with her as one woman with another, rather than as mother and daughter.

However, in the case of her son, she really needs to apply herself in earnest; he is still young and it is up to her to guide him.

So, her attitude with regard to the middle room is to see it as a first small step in resolving the problem of separation from the son. A middle room at many levels, an intermediary passage for both the mother and the young boy.

*

Under the staircase which leads to the upper floor there is a dark closet which, with the passage of time, comes to worry the woman.

She doesn't remember what's inside, she only knows that that dark cavern contains pieces of her previous life in Italy, left and forgotten there in the *annus horribilis*. According to the Feng Shui that she has consulted on more than one occasion, dark corners and things hoarded but unused obstruct the flow of positive energies and that storage closet, crowded with different objects, thrown in there haphazardly and never considered again, creates a blockage in the corridor between the bathroom and the kitchen.

The woman finally opens the small door cautiously one day and, in the dim light that comes through between the wooden planks, discovers her photography enlarger.

She had taken up photography with Silvio when they were married many years ago and wanted to do something interesting together. He had taken it seriously; one could immediately tell that he had an exceptional eye. Not in her case; she had begun to take pictures without that passion or that discipline that would have provided with her a sense of security, with those basic fundamentals from which to begin and from which to be able to derive the pleasure of experimenting.

It was only later, during that year in Kenya with Giacomo when, no longer able to teach in Italy (due to old political issues), that she had again taken up photography, as a means of personal expression and (why not?) as a new possible line of work.

And then the following year, returning from New York to Rome, her encounter with Eleonora, a brilliant photographer, had really aroused her enthusiasm. Alongside Eleonora, after almost two years of living abroad, the woman was seeing Rome through the filter of a lens with a disenchanted eye; for the first time no longer as the centre of her world but rather as the place of shattered dreams of revolution.

Quite a number of former comrades, friends and acquaintances were in prison; many others were licking their wounds, whether with drugs, alcohol or psychoanalysis. Some had taken their own lives, a few had beaten a dignified retreat; others, having come down from their high horse, had chosen to compromise.

She certainly had been no better; she had chosen to flee.

With many excuses, it is true. Her stable relationship with Giacomo, who was being sent abroad for work here and there, her suspension for infringing the code of good behaviour, an enduring legacy of the Fascist era, and thus the end of her teaching career and therefore the necessity, with a little girl in tow, to find a new way of earning a living. But all that said, what she had chosen to do was to flee.

At times she thought she should have stayed, accepted the searing defeat, the repression, the years of lead and, one fish swimming in the same sea as many others, silently engaged in the reconstruction of a long-term project for change.

She reviewed her political past like watching a film in cinemascope:

- the red duffle coat

- the pink Ciao moped on which, at dawn, she would go to

megaphone the female workers in front of the Fatme factory

- the fiery speeches, cheeks flaring with emotion, at the rallies in front of the Literature Faculty at the Sapienza University

- the prison of Rebibbia where she had briefly sojourned three times and left her thumbprint in ink

- the months spent at Gela in Sicily with female and male comrades, hoping for a revolution in Southern Italy

- the return to Rome and the progressive end of her blind faith in Potere Operaio, a political group that she had much loved until then, and her parallel blind faith in an outward change that might not also involve an internal change

- her new-found interest in feminism and the notion of the personal as political, and then *Zizzania*, the ironic and provocative post-feminist magazine which she and her female friends had published and then distributed wearing black lipstick, turbans on their heads and snakes around their necks.

In New York she had taken up photography again. This time the city, magnificent with its skyscrapers and the Twin Towers that could be seen from her apartment, its urban landscape so dramatic and hard-edged, resonated with her defeated and fleeing spirit.

She had then continued doing it in Rome; she had begun, together with Eleanora, photographing the urban landscape and mounting exhibitions such as "EUR-Foro Italico Round Trip", strips of postcards in black and white; "Suspended Tension", photos of roofs and TV antennas in the foreground; then again colour postcards: "The appearance of places, the place of appearances", this time an exhibition of the Roman periphery. She had spent a year on a Vespa with Eleonora, riding around the most desolate neighbourhoods of the city. An unforgettable experience. And finally a super8 film: fast and neurotic images of the centre of Rome, and then very slow and wide-angled shots of the outskirts, in the background a song, a cry of despair and helplessness in the soprano voice of a friend. The super8 was entitled "To have done with Rome". This is how the woman felt at the time.

The lens of the enlarger is very good. She had bought it with Silvio and they used it together to print in black and white. He had subsequently formed a partnership with a talented photographer who unfortunately disappeared a few years later in North Africa, perhaps killed by the mafia or the secret services. So Silvio had decided to continue alone and he had made it, he had become a professional photographer.

But now Silvio wants the lens of the enlarger. He has asked her for it several times and she will take it to him next time she goes to Rome. Which is only right; he is continuing to take photographs, she isn't.

She takes it out of the enlarger, puts it back in the special small blue container, closes the closet without putting anything back in place and takes it upstairs to her pink room.

*

The residents of the castle meet daily in the small lopsided living room with its rectangular table and window facing the garden through which enter, undaunted, the branches of the ever-encroaching ivy. The space is small, one can only sit around the table or in the alcove; the sofa has seen better times and often one has to fight over it with the cats. Originally the kitchen and living room had been separated by an absurd partition which the generous friends making their ad hoc renovations had torn down six years earlier; in its place there's now a square chest that functions as a storage space. The child often uses it as a jumping platform.

Meal times vary and depend on the different school, university and work activities of the various residents.

The child, and consequently the woman, have regular times for breakfast and dinner, the others join if possible, otherwise they cook separately. The daughter is vegetarian, the family friend eats mostly traditional Italian food, the daughter's new boyfriend from the desert trip (a very frequent guest) is flexible. At the moment the child only wants to eat pasta. The woman feels disoriented, unhappy with her job, worried that the child may not be settling in well, that the daughter may no longer be fitting in with them. The new boyfriend, however, fits in well. After an interregnum period, the family friend moves to Redfern and the daughter's boyfriend moves in to Busby.

The dynamics of the castle change with the departure of the family friend. The child, overjoyed at the arrival of a man in his house – at last! – does his best in a thousand ways to make himself loved, including his sister in the emotional circle, sometimes excluding the mother who is happy with the understanding between the children, and also for those unexpected moments of personal freedom.

When there are guests for dinner, however, the daily worries disappear; the woman puts them aside and allows herself a vacation.

Ever since she was small, she has always loved to immerse herself in "the group". The family home was an open house, always many guests for lunch or dinner, relatives and friends who would drop in for a coffee; children who came to play with her and her two brothers; former maids who brought home-made cakes and requested favours. When with others, her innate curiosity has always been able to direct itself towards them, that is, to face outward, instead of sliding, like a sharp knife, inside her where it often discovered dark corners. And among "the others", she forgets herself, she no longer feels alone with her problems but part of an interesting and articulated whole.

In the small living room, in the evenings with guests, everyone crowds around the table, chairs are brought from the other rooms, everyone comes closer together, one or two even eat on the bench or on the sofa. The almost primitive kitchen is spread along the wall opposite the table so that whoever is on cooking duty has to turn their back to the guests, and this at times slows down the preparation of meals, when whoever is cooking wants to participate in the conversation and may even be inclined to stop in the middle of frying something, in order to express their opinion.

The friends are many. Partly because the woman has kept in touch with friends in Sydney from the old days when they were very happy, she, Giacomo and the two children, living, before buying Busby, in the beautiful waterfront apartment on New Beach Road, Darling Point. Partly because in the five years that the woman was in Canberra, the castle has been inhabited by a considerable number of people, of different ages and races, religion, culture and political ideas, all in turn with different friends, all still gravitating, some more and some less, around Busby.

Most of the friends are recent expatriates, often having migrated not out of necessity but by choice, with a very keen interest in Australian politics (as a way of confirming the idea that they were right to move Down Under) and in the politics of their mother country (similarly to confirm the idea that they did well to abandon it).

Many come with terrible stories of political repression in their home countries: there are the South Americans including the Chileans, who have their stories of Allende and Pinochet; the Argentinians, who have seen family and friends forcibly "disappeared"; the Colombians and Brazilians have their stories of drugs and urban violence; the Germans, of course, are finally emerging from the nightmares of Nazism and the Second World War; the Canadians are relaxed and calm, very like the

Australians, and the Italians are still obsessed with the recent events of the Red Brigades and the years of lead.

The Italian expatriates who frequent Busby are all left-leaning even if with different political backgrounds so that, when they meet, they often quarrel. Their past is a delicate tangle, it's their true identity card: I was a member of the PCI; I was never a communist; I was an anarchist; I was in the student movement. I was a supporter of Prima Linea, I was catholic but a dissenter.

The woman often takes issue with the Italians. There are myriad political stances and they are all very different. And then she discovers that none of her friends have participated as actively in the political events of recent years as she and Giacomo have. Very few come from Rome. Everyone loves to have their say, become heated, get involved, argue. All, however, love Sydney and Australia. All love to recount, and often to recount again and again, their own personal story. Everyone feels good in the castle which seems to welcome and nourish this diversity. Busby has been witness to so much; its walls come from the rocks of the ancient hill on which it stands, nothing can daunt it and perhaps the residents and the friends of the residents feel this reassuring energy.

(VOICES OFF)

... that some had left Italy because they had become disillusioned with the fractured dreams of revolution and wanted to venture to a place as far as possible from the place of political defeat, that they wanted to live in the natural wilderness and wanted to learn about Aboriginal culture and the Aboriginal people, the oldest living population in the world, that they had arrived in Australia after travelling all over Asia and also through the Pacific islands, that they had met their great Australian love somewhere else but at a later time had joined up in Sydney, that they were gay and didn't fit in well at home, that Australia was less homophobic than their country, that they had come for work and then remained, that they had become enchanted by the natural environment here and could no longer go back to their polluted cities, that here it was easy to find work and a place to live, that here they could finally learn English, that they had no regrets because Sydney was so open, multicultural, full of people who came from all over the world, that many different languages were spoken in Australia which are culturally enriching in contrast to that antiquated world from which they came and in which nothing ever changed, that they had left their families behind because there were often painful and unresolved issues, that they felt free to do and be whatever they wanted and what they had not been able to do elsewhere, that one could dress as one wanted instead of having to follow stupid fads, that here there was a respect for nature that on the other side of the world people couldn't even imagine, that the beaches were all free and the parks provided their own barbeque areas, that here everyone, from the worker to the billionaire, went to the pub all together in thongs, that corruption and the mafia did not exist here, that the police only appeared when necessary and, moreover, were more like well-educated and smiling parking officers, that driving licences didn't require a photo and that one didn't need to show an identity card, that dealing with the bureaucracy was a walk in the park and the organisation of the society was efficient but relaxed, that in order to stay in Australia it was enough to marry a friend and live together for some time, that young people could leave their family at 18 because they immediately found work and housing, that the dole was easy to get and enough to live on, if only modestly, that a city like Sydney, where the sea was pristine even with four million inhabitants, had parks available around every corner, easy access to public swimming pools, the weather was always good even in winter, how wonderful it all was!

*

It's March, in the evening.

The living room is crowded, guests overflow onto the small veranda, into the alcove, even into the corridor and the two gardens. The cooks are busy despite the heat and the mosquitoes; heated discussions are in the air; an argument or two about the pasta, quickly resolved because it is finally cooked al dente, so everyone to the table.

In front of the steaming plates, the Italians are quick to speak their minds: it's very good, it's missing a bit of salt, my mother made it like this, my grandmother made it like that; there is nothing better than a plate of spaghetti when you are waiting.

The others – Chinese French South-American German English Indonesian (and more) – smile politely. All, however, continually turn to look at the television.

There's an anticipatory silence which, little by little, becomes more tense, more worrying, then chilling, as the election results scroll down the screen and the journalists throw themselves at the data like hyenas ready to devour the victim at hand. Meanwhile the chatter resumes.

The woman has spent five years in the Australian capital enjoying watching with her friends the parliamentary debates broadcast late at night on TV. Paul Keating has succeeded in getting her interested in politics again with his passion, his grasp of the big picture, and his lightning, caustic wit. His opponents tremble. To her mind, even if not as perfect as she would have liked, he has nevertheless been a good prime minister. Many Australians, however, consider him "arrogant" and for this reason they have not elected him again today, preferring the liberal John Howard, a man, some might say, without qualities. He had not expected to win and now there's a fear that he will overturn all the positive measures that Keating had introduced, and those of Bob Hawke before him. It's been 13 years of a Labor federal government, exciting years marked by multiculturalism, environmental protection, recognition of the Aboriginal people as the first inhabitants of Australia, free universities, agreements between trade unions and employers – all since 1983, the fateful year when she had arrived in Australia and life was beautiful. It's a terrible turn of events, she can't even think about it; a great collective shock, no one was prepared for this change. Theories, criticisms, quarrels, heated arguments. Then, little by little, silence.

The warm subtropical night seduces the souls and fatigue descends; everyone gets to their feet, silently traverses the long dark corridor and at the front door all embrace, friends again.

*

She really does not like the long, poorly-lit narrow corridor.

The more she walks through it, the less she likes it; it is perhaps the only part of the castle that just doesn't go down well with her.

The woman has always loved Italian entrances, the intervening space between the outside and the inside; the place of ceremonies, of welcome, of hugs and kisses, of chocolates and flowers offered up to the hosts. Guests stop there for a moment in order to acclimatise themselves to the inside, to the energies of the people who live there.

The entrance hall at viale Pinturicchio in Rome, many moons ago in her parents' house, was one of her favourite rooms. Bright and square with a large bevelled mirror, an English George V coffee table and two gilded candelabra, its marble floor extending to the right into the sitting room and to the left into the dining room, both rooms connected with the entrance hall by two large glass doors.

There she and her brother, when they were very small, had invented their first game: "turn turn turn", and they would spin like dervishes, with arms raised to shoulder height, singing at the top of their voices: *abballerinabandierarossatrionferà*, until their heads were really spinning and they fell, gleefully, to the ground.

For important events, lunches and dinners, the two doors were opened completely and, together with the entrance in the middle, the three rooms became a single large hall. Adjacent to the front door was a small dressing room with an antique coat rack that included a mirror, a place for umbrellas and even a narrow shelf for the black, bulky telephone. It was the place of confessions in the dark, of unexpected revelations, the place where everything was allowed, even the most intimate of secrets. She sought refuge there in order to speak on the phone with her young girlfriends and, later, with her young suitors.

In Australia, instead of an entrance hall, the early houses built by the invaders and closely modelled on those of the motherland, open for the most part on narrow and long corridors that one enters in single file and then walks briskly up to the first room. Every time she traverses the corridor, the woman imagines possible, and more often impossible, changes to that dark bowel that connects the front, the back, the above and the below of Busby. She talks about it with friends who are knowledgeable about architecture, friends who are photographers or visionaries. There are diverse and heated opinions; at times she even considers tearing down the hundred-year-old wall between the corridor and the first room and making the resulting space a single area. It would certainly be much brighter, but also, undoubtedly, a foolhardy move.

This morning, however, she has had an idea that perhaps will reconcile her with the hated corridor. Walking up and down in front of Hyde Park with a friend, she had seen a young Italian street artist drawing a Madonna by Leonardo, whom she had always loved so much. Of course, a Madonna would be out of place on the corridor wall and would not solve the problem that is close to her heart but, just but, if the boy – and she had got him to give her his phone number – were as good as he seemed to be, if the boy, that is, were capable, he might be able to paint her a trompe-l'oeil on the wall with a false perspective. For example, a veranda overlooking the sea with a bright sky and a little boat in the distance.

She goes up and down the corridor, looks at the chosen wall from various angles, imagines the painting and tries to understand how and where the false perspective should be in order to be seen at its best. Because, of course, the corridor is a passageway, so the perspective changes as you move along it. Should the illusion, then, be seen from the entrance or in the middle of the corridor, or at the end? Or even as you retrace your steps upon leaving? At this point, the woman is overtaken by a whirlwind of possibilities and, as often happens, she cannot help but get lost in the meanders and pathways of the mind, that lead her to new crossroads, located in more and more distant areas; other possibilities, ever more impossible, leading almost to the loss of reason before even beginning to reason. But in this loss of oneself, there is a sort of enjoyment, a return to childhood, to the days when she spoke to herself and invented stories with plots which unfurled through images ever more unmoored from that Once Upon a Time there was a Little Girl, a girl who was, of course the woman herself who was forever getting lost.

At this point, then, she goes into the kitchen and makes a bancha tea in which she places an umeboshi plum in order to regain an operational balance for the advancing day.

*

The wooden stairs had been painted dark brown by friends always in that distant and painful period.

It's a colour, however, that the woman does not like at all. It's too gloomy for her and she would have liked to strip the paint and return the wood to its warm and protective natural honey colour, but with so much else to do and unable to use her hands as she would have liked, she has quickly given up on the idea.

In another life, manual skills would certainly have come before all those useless and harmful notions instilled in her when she was a child about the mind, which was the ruling class, and the arms and physical labour, namely the working class.So much so that now she is always fearful and apprehensive when she needs to do anything with her hands. Cooking, (cuttingpeelingfryingboilingbakingkneadingcrumbing), now that's something she likes a lot but for everything else she's all thumbs. Thinking about doing things, now she's very good at that; but then putting into action what she has thought, is always difficult. And so the stairs, as she goes up and down them many times a day, are the subject of careful reflections on how perhaps … if only she wanted to … might be returned to their former glory.

But then, beneath it all, there is always the loophole of imagining that one day in the future, using her share of the family inheritance, divided three ways between her and her brothers, she may be able to carry out the much-fantasised renovation of the entire castle.

The castle is certainly in dire need of it. It's falling apart in many places; a lack of convenience is its characteristic tone and a dearth of light in various areas its other notable feature. So, should she embark on an enterprise for which she lacks the competence and therefore does not know what results she might obtain? Scraping the paint from the stairs, filling the holes, sanding, applying the primer, then the oil, letting it dry and then polishing the steps one by one (but not too much because there's the risk of someone breaking their neck) – all this when, everything considered, the renovation would bring with it the replacement of that old staircase with a more modern one, one with open steps that would allow a glimpse of the living room area, with its planned grand window overlooking the sea, instead of that dark blotch blocking the light at the front of the castle. Would all this be worth the trouble?

But, for now, she, the boy, the daughter, the overnight guests, the renters, the visiting relatives, the dear friends, and even the cats go up and down, up and down. Everyone continues to use that old dark brown staircase, as it leads upstairs to the bedrooms and downstairs to the bathroom, the kitchen, the veranda, the living room and the entrance hall.

It is, the woman says to console herself, good physical exercise.

Up and down, as in life. At least that's how her life has been.

A continuous change of perspective, of vision, of reflection, many times a day.

*

Fourth of June, in the evening.

She hasn't wanted a big party for her fiftieth birthday.

She has approached it with trepidation. She has decided to return to Sydney from Canberra before the big event; half her life – perhaps even more – already over; better to take decisions now rather than postpone them to an unpredictable future.

Leaving Canberra hadn't been easy. She had nursed her grief there for five years. There the little boy had been happy with his closest friend, with the beautiful garden at Hovea Street and his sunny room full of games; there at the Australian National University she had finally found some great professional satisfactions.

But … and there is often a but in her life. It had weighed on her more than a little to have left her daughter just at the point of her coming of age in Sydney with her family friend, there in the castle of broken dreams, gone to rack and ruin. She knew that in Canberra, alone and with a small child, in a small Australian town, certainly the seat of the federal government but still not very multicultural and mainly centred on Australian politics and the research university, she had felt cramped.

The woman had always lived, in Italy and abroad, in big cities where she could lose herself in the crowd and feel anonymous if she wanted. In Canberra, on the other hand, everywhere she went she would meet colleagues, students, friends, all connected with the university, which meant her work. At times she felt almost imprisoned in her role as an academic, a constricting and repetitive dimension that she had always shunned. Given all this, her return to Sydney had been the logical outcome.

But now that she is back in Sydney, and has settled down as she wanted and only needs to concentrate on life in the present, every now and then as she looks from the windows of her pink room at the infinite expanse of the sea below her, a furtive thought, almost forbidden, even if long-standing and recurrent, comes into her mind. It's the idea of returning to Rome, to the fold, which often erupts in her entangled imaginings. Her extended family is there; her two dear brothers, sisters-in-law, nephew and nieces, cousins and many, still so many, friends. Why doesn't she just pull up stakes and go back? What is it that really keeps her here, in this very remote country, forgotten by God and men, where she happened to land by chance and where things have gone exactly in the opposite direction to what she had expected?

And here the answer that she often gives herself like an old refrain, even if perhaps not complete, leaps to her heart. It's because she must settle what she had left suspended. Busby. It could have been their "love nest", a place to watch their children grow, to create a safe cradle from which to expand their knowledge in myriad directions, as he, and she also, would have liked to do, freely without prejudices, nor ideology, nor any provincialism of any sort. On their own, free and happy.

Instead here it is, the castle, a crumbling cavern even if full of atmosphere. The woman looks at the living room, the kitchen, the alcove with a critical eye; there is much to do, who knows if she will make it.

And yet ... no use thinking about it now; today is her celebration and worries are better left to another day. She manages, as usual, to distract herself from the problem that assails her and to concentrate on whatever pleasantries the evening can offer.

Her children, the daughter's boyfriend, the family friend, a couple of young and congenial friends have prepared a delicious dinner, with dessert about to come. The friend suddenly disappears, the others hold back the cake and candles, the woman doesn't understand.

Suddenly there is a knock on the door. No one offers to go, they insist that she go. Disgruntled, she walks down the corridor while a great deal of shouting can be heard from outside. She pulls open the door and in the darkness of the night sees a line of friends winding from the corner of the street to the entrance of Busby, each with a bright sparkler in their hand, each singing Happy Birthday!

The castle comes alive, the quiet evening turns into a bright, boisterous party filled with gifts, with music, with dancing, hugs. The door that leads to the back garden opens wide to accommodate the overflow of friends, now too tightly crowded into the little veranda. Up and down the stairs there's a great coming and going; the sparkling wine is opened, another large cake, speeches are made, she also speaks, moved, and declares herself happy, yes, truly happy, now in this precise moment, for the tormented choice to remain in Australia, in spite of everything.

She looks around and finds everything and everyone suddenly marvellous. She is amazed and enchanted by the affection of so many friends. Life in Sydney, at Busby, life itself, seems beautiful to her again.

She launches into the future half of her life with a smile.

"Dancing, I feel like dancing into infinity" she writes in one of her poems.

*

The bathroom is one of the many sore points of the house.

Not because it's ugly, far from it! Narrow and long with a large window, the decadent and scuffed tub with lion paws, the high copper ceiling worked in curlicues but unfortunately painted white; it has a solemn air that befits the castle. It needs, however, a total restoration, it has probably never been touched since the beginning of time.

The washbasin is absolutely not to her taste. Installed there by the generous friends, who *in illo tempore* had attempted to carry out the ad hoc renovations, it has a shape that the woman detests; it's a solid block, the basin itself is tiny, practically useless, and with an ugly attached cabinet. A far cry from the very beautiful, large, spacious ceramic washbasins to which she had been accustomed in Italy, as in her parent's house, a column that rose from the floor to support the dish, in which she could almost fully wash herself if she didn't want to shower. Nothing as exotic as the bucket with which she had washed herself outside her hut facing the coral reef at Kiriwina, in the Trobriand Islands. And certainly nothing as artistic as the 1920s sink situated under the window of her New York bathroom, with a slice of the metropolis visible from the window. At Busby, a washbasin without qualities.

The shower in the bathtub with lion's paws at Busby is also inconvenient and malfunctioning. The walls are discoloured and the floor is a repainted concrete, everywhere peeling off and revealing, almost as in a Pollock painting, dark stains underneath, sometimes a dirty white, sometimes bottle-green, sometimes almost black.

The condensation that forms after a shower is a serious problem in winter. Without an extractor fan, the bathroom fills with an impenetrable fog that cannot be dispersed except by throwing open the large window exposed to the winds that come up from the sea.

At the bathroom entrance, next to the door, there is a sort of open closet, always the handiwork of those friends in the past, covered by a colourful sarong, in which the inhabitants of Busby throw suitcases and rarely used objects which, obviously, don't benefit from the humidity created by the various morning ablutions.

In the morning, the woman locks herself in the bathroom for a long uncomfortable shower in the bathtub with lion's paws. In her dreams, the bathroom is a recurring image, a place of very strange and unlikely encounters; there is always water flowing and this, she has read, must represent the movement of her emotions which emerge and unfold before her eyes. Positive dreams then, she hopes.

And so from there, from that damp hole, from that bathroom so different from all those she has known in the past, naked and assailed by sea winds, the woman examines her life and what to do in the near future. She lingers as long as she can, allowing herself to be caressed by the always boiling water, letting herself be lulled by the fragments of her dreams.

She only emerges from her torpor when there's a knock at the door. Her shift is over, it's someone else's turn.

*

The downstairs room immediately on the left after the entrance is quite lovely.

A square of medium size, it has a wall with triple windows that illuminate the whole room. The woman settles in there soon after the family friend moves to Redfern and the daughter, with the new boyfriend from her trip to the desert, decides to take the large bedroom upstairs. The woman prefers to go downstairs; she imagines that the two young sweethearts may feel freer without the girl's mother nearby and she hopes the son may become more independent. The pink room thus becomes the room for the always numerous guests.

The woman feels a special energy in the downstairs room, an energy that now she calls, without any problem, spiritual, because she no longer gets it confused with the religion of her ancestors which she renounced during her years of rebellion in Rome. Instead, she draws this energy from her rapport with Aboriginal culture which, even if only recently, has enchanted her with its oral dream stories which create the world, with songs that show the way, a treading of the earth with a light step. And also from the oriental disciplines which she had already begun to explore some time before moving to Southeast Asia. The conjunction of Yin and Yang now interests her much more strongly than the dichotomy of Good and Evil of Catholic lore.

The energy in the downstairs room gives her the strength to finally create a morning routine of meditation and yoga in succession. The woman has always been unable to establish continuity, one of her major failings, but this space, so open to the outside world, to the orange tree that bears fruit twice a year, resonates well with her newfound love of physical and mental discipline.

A round, slightly bulging pillow under her bottom, a small yoga mat for her crossed legs, back straight, early in the morning before the rush, breakfast, son to school, she to work. A brief look at the window and what lies beyond, then eyes closed, breathing under control, sensations throughout the body, breathing again, slowly.

The Vipassana meditation allows her to start the day well, makes her feel in harmony with herself. She manages, in that interval of stillness, to accept herself, something which has been always difficult for her in the past. It allows her to feel all one and not broken into many parts, to understand that the breath that circulates throughout her body and then comes out and mixes with the breath of the world, is the breath of Life that continually renews itself and can make her change her relationship to herself and to others. Twenty minutes later, yoga.

Removing the pillow, with bare feet on the small blue mat, the woman recreates the positions which, twice a week, she enthusiastically learns in the classes at Randwick taught by her brilliant teacher, Dee, who is also greatly admired by the woman's talented daughter who does yoga every day. The woman has always been physically active; from a young age she liked to run, she was very fast and often even beat the boys. As a teenager she had participated in student championships and in high school she had been part of a basketball team and competed against other schools. Then her political activism, the smoke-filled classrooms, the couches on which endless discussions took place, the joints, all had pushed physical exercise into the far horizon. Now she wants to begin again; she has a garden full of trees, the park with the beach and the sea below her house. She is quitting smoking; she lives in a country where fitness is central to people's lives, she cannot hold back. Among the many possible activities, she has chosen yoga because it resonates best with her interest in the connections between the body, the mind, the environment and the universe. In truth, yoga is Hindu while Vipassana meditation is Buddhist, but it doesn't matter; she now loves mixing things, creating hybrids, messing about in this multicultural world in which she finds herself living. Everything makes some sort of sense in the vast space of Australia and she can at times forget the linear time she was accustomed to in the old world from which she has come. And so the woman feels ready to face the day.

*

The laundry is the place for trash

- of what is useless – although one never knows

- of old things to be given away but that forever accumulate

- of broken things awaiting mending

- of I don't remember whose this is, but someone will eventually come back to get it

- of bottles to be recycled

- of extra supplies overflowing from the kitchen

- of clothes to be washed, always too many to do at once

- of a washing machine often not working

- of less important souvenirs to be given away or taken to Vinnies

- of the cat basket in which, however, the cats never sleep

- of garden tools that are always too little used

- of chairs, small tables, deckchairs

the laundry is the basement

- a dark cave full of mystery

- it's the support and the ultimate root of the castle

- the pillars on which everything rests

- the foundations.

The woman is frightened of it and goes there very little, her excuse being that she doesn't like washing clothes.

When she was little she loved looking out of the window of her room in viale Pinturicchio at Angela, their Calabrian laundress, who, once a week, in the large granite tub on the balcony, would beat, wring, spread, spot clean, soap, rinse and re-rinse the sheets, a task that Lina, the maid, refused to do. Angela always sang when she washed. Lina, who found her annoying, would insinuate that perhaps Angela was drunk; she certainly laughed too much for her liking. There was no laundry in viale Pinturicchio but that corner of the narrow and long kitchen balcony with the granite tub dedicated to the sheets was a special place for her as a child, and later as a teenager. It was a cheerful place; they spoke through the window, she and Angela, who would tell her about her own mother, the illegitimate daughter of local nobles down there in Calabria, forced to marry a peasant in an obscure mountain village. The woman would later go and visit Angela there, after the first student demonstrations, during a summer spent with her friend, Clara.

Opening onto the first level of the back garden, the Busby laundry enjoys a magnificent view of the sea toward Coogee, with the honeysuckle hedge to the right, a tree fern directly in front, slightly further down a palm tree and on the left a delicate tree with beautiful flowers the colour of damask plums.

The parties, the mythical Busby parties, inevitably spill out into the back garden, which is quite large and which, with its three levels, allows for the privacy of intimate conversations, of fleeting kisses, and of special joints only shared between connoisseurs. It's there that on hot and humid summer nights one ends up listening to the last of the music, talking about everything and more than everything, drinking those last staggering toasts, letting out those resentments, those loves, those hopes for a better future.

The woman, in those evenings teeming with friends, dares to venture into the harshly-lit laundry without fear and puts on the washing machine.

*

The narrow side lane that winds down along the left of the castle and goes down to the laundry, the back garden and from there to the two garages, has undergone continual changes.

Originally bare dirt and later paved with bricks, it is often treated as a depot for building materials sometime needed to repair lopsided windows or rotten wooden floorboards. At times one comes across a half-used can of paint or an abandoned children's bike.

Then there's the age-old problem of the small gate to the left of the castle. It was soon discovered that the one already in place was so rotted through that it could hardly stand. She and Giacomo hadn't noticed it, all excited as they had been at the prospect of buying their own Australian home (and at an auction, no less, a novelty for the young Italians that they were). The small gate had thus been an insignificant detail, probably always open in the two hasty visits they had made to the property before deciding to buy it, fascinated by its mystery and its decadence.

Later, with the child always wanting to open and close everything, the woman decided to change at least the latch. She took the decision but then continually postponed it: there were too many other important things to be fixed that claimed priority, so for a long time a piece of rope was used to close it and so safeguard the child from possible sorties onto the road.

Now that the child has grown, the small gate remains always open and, using the path, the cats from the neighbouring houses constantly venture into the back garden to go and raid the generously-filled food bowls of Coco and Cosmo.

If, one small step at a time, one manages to get down to the entrance of the first garage and turns around to look up, the castle reveals itself in all its majesty and its decay. The rear part is the most ruined: added later, it's made of highly perishable material. Exposed as it is to the ravages of the southern winds that sometimes buffet it with relentless violence, it nevertheless affords a glimpse of the beauty of the sandstone of the front part.

Like an ancient jewel, half-hidden and overladen with dust, just waiting to be rediscovered, cleaned and restored to the splendour it deserves.

*

The garages are accessed either via a small door that opens onto the third and last level of the back garden or from the lane that runs along the southern perimeter of the castle grounds.

The half-broken shutters cannot be properly locked. Inside, the garage on the left remains in total darkness while the one on the right lets in some light from the low door that opens onto the garden. The two garages look like witches' caverns and one needs to hold the shutters open if one wants to see inside. Garaging the car itself is too complicated. In order to reach the house, one would have to go back up the garden, perhaps at night in the dark, perhaps lugging heavy shopping bags. Better, then, to park at the front on Busby Parade.

The garages contain large objects: things you no longer want to use or can't use yet, things that you should give away but can't find anyone who wants them, or things that you don't want to sell or throw away just yet. It also houses other people's belongings, stored there for various reasons and waiting to be retrieved. Now and then, the left garage is rented or used as a sort of art workshop by the daughter or by various friends and acquaintances. The one on the right, instead, always remains a storage space and only occasionally is opened for a garage sale for which owners and friends gather everything in there that they want to get rid of.

The humidity, the cobwebs and what may be mice, discourage individual but favour group visits, which usually take place after a hearty Sunday lunch when some guest brings new items to store or remembers something to take away.

For the woman the garages are a place of memory, of dormant memories that suddenly return, of what might have been, in the darkness of the heart that at times prevails.

She often has to pass by them when going for a walk along the sea-cliff, the seven-kilometre round trip from Bronte to Bondi, the path rising and falling with an ocean below that is sometimes serene and sometimes tumultuous. Gingerly, she raises the shutter and begins to observe from a distance what is left of her past life, especially

- her daughter's Swedish wall bars, bought from a former student in Rome and much used by the girl for doing acrobatics in their small, beautiful apartment in Vicolo Jandolo in Trastevere

- Giacomo's golf clubs, a gift from a colleague in Nairobi, where he had never been able to initiate them due to a mother cheetah calving in hole number 9 of the golf course near their resort, the Milimani Hotel

- Great-aunt Clementina's round bevelled-mirror coffee-table with its ivy-leaf legs. It was a small table that she had often admired in the living room of via Donatello, together with the burgundy velvet armchairs and the sliding wooden doors with hunting scenes, the work of a Bulgarian painter friend of her great-uncle on her mother's side, Mikail Mikailoff.

The woman then pulls the shutter down and with it closes off her memories. She looks around and recognises the light, the heat, the colours of Sydney. She heads for the cliff.

*

The facade of the castle is made of honed sandstone. Large slabs, perhaps transported by hand by the two stonemason brothers, they are lit by the sun in the morning and the millennial sand seems to ooze from the walls. The lacy windows give it all an imposing gothic appearance.

At times, walking back from the sea, the woman pauses to look at what is now her home from the distance and compares it in memory with all those dwellings where she has already lived

In Rome:

- the house in via Firenze, where she was born and where her destiny was decided

- the house in viale Pinturicchio where, as an adolescent, she wrote down her dreams and her secrets in the diary dedicated to Anne Frank

- the house in via Bevagna where she spent the major part of her political years, still in the womb of her family

- the house at Grottarossa with the large terrace in the middle of the pines that saw the birth of her beloved little girl and the brief years of happiness with her first husband

- the house at Ponte Milvio, a house that witnessed the disintegration of her marriage, and her years of feminism

- the house at Trastevere with the fourteenth-century courtyard invaded in spring by the blooming wisteria, the terrace overlooking the Orange Garden and the fateful meeting with Giacomo

In Nairobi:

- the residence with the giant jacaranda tree and the swimming pool surrounded by, what were for her, exotic flowers; the hot potato chips and hamburger for the little girl, "mtoto" in Swahili; the club for "Blacks Only", where she danced in the middle of the dance floor with her friend, Tommy, after smoking a huge joint with weed bought at the Nairobi fruit market

In New York:

- the apartment on Fifth Avenue, corner of Fourteenth, from which the Twin Towers and Washington Square could be seen shimmering in the evening as the Italian political exiles gathered in the dining room to plot and talk, talk and talk some more

In Algiers:

- the little villa outside the Kasbah with orange trees and the couscous handmade by Sahra, the cleaning lady

In Sydney:

- the art deco apartment on New Beach Road from where, at dawn, she would take photos of the harbour and the skyscrapers, and where she had been romantically, deliriously happy

- the terrace house in Paddington where the teenage daughter had managed to half destroy the living room with a wild party, and where the little boy, for those few months, still enjoyed the immeasurable affection of his already-sick father

- the houses they briefly lived in, in Ilona and Armando's place in Paddington, in Joan's apartment in Rose Bay, in Bronte at Mona and Paul's before the via crucis to the hospitals, and while waiting for generous friends to fix even minimally, the serious problems in the castle they had just bought

In Canberra:

- the beautiful house in Canberra, a well-kept cottage from the 1950s, surrounded by a magnificent garden where plants of all kinds would grow out of all proportion, and which had been a peaceful five-year interlude before returning to Busby where she now lives and at times wonders for how long.

*

And so, life goes on

Between one electricity bill

Feeding the cats

The sauce with sautéed garlic

The son to drive here and there

A hurried phone call to the daughter

Applying lipstick in the rear-view mirror at traffic lights.

A period of relative calm descends on Busby and its residents. Having left the Catholic University after a year with no regrets, the woman is happy at Sydney University where she had already worked before getting the position at the Australian National University in Canberra.

Among the rediscovered former colleagues and friends, many who, like her, had expatriated in the 1980s but not out of economic necessity, she notes some points in common, some differences. Being the only one to have engaged in full-time political activity in her homeland, the woman always attempts to bring to her work that spark of idealism, that utopian political vision that had shaped her and accustomed her to go beyond her personal interests in the attempt to envisage, and have others envisage, a better society. Thus, every piece of research, every presentation, is an opportunity to inspire students to imagine a Possible Path, to help them to dare and to hope.

She is also thinking of creating an educational radio program suitable for each school and university level, in order to replace the textbook with authentic materials produced, at least partially, by the students themselves. It will be called RadioActive. In short, she now feels the return of positive energy and, with it, the desire to experiment.

In Australia she is eager to highlight what had so enthused her and Giacomo on their arrival:

- the multiculturalism, this new model of relations between races, languages and cultures, at this point unique in the world and therefore precious and forward-looking to her mind, stuffed full, as she is, of European "No Future" slogans

- the militant environmentalism of the Australian Greens, who oppose the presence of the gigantic US navy ships in Sydney Harbour on their colourful surfboards. Their protests have already prevented the construction of a large dam in the wilderness of Tasmania and their boycotts of the large supermarkets which still don't stock organic products have attracted much publicity, as have their attacks on the multinationals regarding their GM products

- the new relationship opening up with the indigenous population with whom a number of treaties have been signed so that, even if the road may be long, there are hopes that a Reconciliation might be possible with the Australian First People.

The daughter is happy with her boyfriend who is the son of close family friends and who finds himself at ease at Busby with all of them, creating an atmosphere which is both pleasant and relaxed. Together, both he and the daughter, have decided to make a documentary about Roxby Downs, the uranium mine in South Australia which they had encountered on their trip through the Simpson Desert. They have made contact with the Arabana Aboriginal group, the custodians of that area, and they want to spend time with them. Having managed to secure funding from the Australian Film Commission for the project, they are full of enthusiasm. The daughter is also finishing her Bachelor of Fine Arts at UNSW. She is making progress in her studies; the mother sees that the essays she has to write and the presentations she has to make are helping her mature. She is very pleased with the result.

The son, on the other hand, is not the least interested in studying. He only likes the cinema for which, it seems, he has a keen eye. And then there's his overwhelming and total passion for soccer, in which he excels and which connects him with his grandfather, a professional player, and his father, in his time a junior player for Roma, the team the son loves. He feels that this is the family tradition and that he must carry it on. The mother is proud of his skill on the field but she fears that it will be at the expense of his academic achievements. She's uncertain of what to do: to accept her son's inclinations or attempt to guide him toward a more academic route?

As usual, she puts it off to another time.

*

Late autumn afternoon, an air of festive expectation at the entrance to Busby.

The woman returns from the airport with her teenage niece and nephew visiting from Rome. Ruggero and Alessia are respectively 15 and 16 years old; they will spend their school holidays in Sydney in order to improve their English.

After meeting their Australian cousins, after the effusive greetings, the organised tour of the castle, visits to the front and back gardens, to the garages, to the pink room where they will settle themselves, at sunset the woman takes them to the Bondi Pavilion. Together with her family friend, her young son all excited by the new arrivals, the daughter with her boyfriend and even two Italian colleagues who have come to visit, they are going to participate in a special event to celebrate the winter solstice. This could be a taste of Sydney's Eastern Suburbs New Age lifestyle for the two young Italians, an interesting exotic experience for them, she thinks. The invocation to the four Archangels at the four corners of the Pavilion, an invocation intended, according to the enthusiastic organisers, to draw down positive energy on the participants on the night of the solstice – something accepted by Bondi Beach goers as just one of the many religious / spiritual / folkloric / cultural events organised at the Pavilion – provokes scepticism in the Italian group. After an initial surprise, the youngest of them find the experience almost comical. The nephew withdraws into a corner with his young cousin who copies him; the niece and her cousin follow, giggling at the orders of the masters of ceremonies; the others can't wait for it all to end. The woman, for some time now caught between two languages and two cultures, well understands the Italians but also understands the Australians.

Australia is very different from Italy. On the way home the woman repeats it to herself once again and she concludes that she feels grateful to her adopted land for having released her from notions inculcated by a monoculture and a canonical religion. She had thrown away her Catholicism together with the bourgeois norms, the cashmere sweaters and the pearl necklace during her second year of an arts degree at La Sapienza University in Rome, when she had become passionate about politics and Marxism had become her new religion. Multicultural life in Australia and, above all, her contact with indigenous culture, have opened up new perspectives for reflection. The love and ecological respect of the first inhabitants of this ancient continent for Mother Earth, their Songlines, which recount it minutely with all its rivers, its animals, its plants, its springs, songs that thus allow one to know a place in detail without having ever seen it, ever having been there, songs that regard the individual not as separate and as master but as one with the environment, the Earth, the Sky, the Universe. These have led her to understand that being a human does not mean being at the centre of the world but being a part of it and a small part at that.

The house livens up with the arrival of the two teenagers, aged halfway between her two children. The pink room little by little fills up with clothes, paintbrushes, canvases, books, notebooks. Alessia goes to bed late and wakes up late; Ruggero is quite the opposite. They only meet up for meals, she helps with the cooking, he washes the dishes; they argue a bit but they are very close. The days quickly fly by.

They bring with them from Italy a breath of Rome that the family, now Down Under, hankers after and always remembers with nostalgia. The comparisons between the here and there are present, the differences are acknowledged, argued for and then are better understood. This is a happy time at Busby; all the young people give new energy to the house, and to the woman, who functions well in the company of others.

Towards the end of their stay, the daughter decides to go to Byron Bay for a short vacation and takes her cousin, Alessia, with her, while Ruggero stays in Sydney with his aunt and his younger cousin.

*

A beautiful sunny winter's day.

At the entrance to Busby are the woman with her heart in her throat, next to her, her nephew Ruggero, the little boy constantly restless, and the family friend. They are waiting; they are all distraught. Finally the car arrives. The daughter and the niece, Alessia, alight, back from Byron Bay, after being picked up at the train station by the daughter's boyfriend.

The mother approaches her daughter. She is emotional, and speaks in a broken voice. It is one of the most difficult moments of her life. The daughter realises that something terrible has happened.

They hurry up the stairs. As soon as they reach the large bright bedroom, the daughter immediately sees on the dresser a lovely photo of her father surrounded by candles, incense, and flowers. Everyone gathers round her, they are all crying. The daughter understands. With her face reddening she sobs "Daddy … my Daddy…". The mother hugs her while the daughter cries in despair. She gathers all her young wits about her and decides she must leave for Italy to attend her father's funeral. The mother begins to organise the departure. The daughter's passport has expired and needs to be renewed immediately. The relatives in Italy are informed of her imminent arrival. The mother's best friend, Patricia, arrives shortly after by plane from Canberra and joins the group who then scuttle in a taxi between the Italian Consulate, the Australian Immigration Office and the bank. The daughter has closed herself off in a deadly silence, the cheeks of her beautiful heart-shaped face will remain flushed until she reaches Rome. The mother busies herself frenetically, continuously talking and babbling. At lunchtime they stop off at Bondi, go on to the beach, sit on benches and eat fish and chips while looking out at the sea in silence.

Words are superfluous.

The mother, the daughter and the young boy will be going while the niece and the nephew will remain in Sydney to complete their courses in English and in painting. They will be under the care of the daughter's boyfriend and the family friend, who has temporarily returned to the castle.

Busby sees off the group departing in the evening, a tragic night for those who stay and for those who go.

*

The small glassed-in veranda is a multipurpose space, a passageway between the ground floor and the back garden, providing access to the laundry and the garages.

For friends it is a much-loved place, often chosen for intimate confessions. The round table and a few lopsided chairs create an atmosphere of openness, reinforced by the ample view of the outside.

It's there that the I Ching is read, horoscopes are cast, ciphers and the oracles of the Cumaean Sibyl are interpreted. The veranda has always been the centrepiece of the parties at Busby where, at a certain point in the evening, everyone gathers, everyone crowds in, with the door that leads downstairs always open for any eventuality. The evening conversations never seem to end. Everyone stays until late; horizons widen, dreams are made with half-open eyes given the late hour. Sometimes regrets but generally hopes prevail, wine and other substances encourage tears and fits of laughter, and for the last ones to leave there is no rush, there is always something more to say.

The woman retreats there every evening after her return from Rome. The daughter has remained in Italy to mourn, to be mollycoddled by their large Italian family and to take care of her father's bequests; the son and the two teenage cousins are upstairs, chatting before going to bed. Down there the woman has access to the telephone and to the kitchen for a cup of tea. It is there that she has some time all for herself, apart from her role as mother, as aunt, as teacher. The little veranda is an enclosed and sheltered place but open to the outside, to the garden and to the sea in the distance; it's the place that most of all in Busby opens her heart and welcomes her emotions. There her diary fills up every evening with reflections, every morning with dreams.

The tragic untimely death of her first husband has left a deep scar inside her. She thinks back over their life together, such a long time ago now, to the birth of their daughter, to the love between them then transformed into friendship, to the last trip together to Bali, the daughter happy to spend time with her father, the little boy very taken with that kind man, so good with children and as passionate about soccer as he is. She feels guilty for not having been able to love him as he perhaps might have wanted, for having then shifted her affections to another, for having failed to encourage him, just a few months before his death, to stay in Australia where he was visiting and where he had the daughter who could have given him a reason for living. She knows that feeling guilty is part of the mourning.

Now she worries about her daughter; this is a hard blow for such a young woman. The woman hopes her daughter's natural fortitude may help her overcome this ordeal. She will try to help her in any way possible.

*

Summer dinner in the back garden, live music.

After a few months in Italy with her large, loving and welcoming family, her daughter returns to Sydney to finish university and to reconnect with her boyfriend.

The atmosphere is warm, everyone is around her, everyone tries to make her understand how close they feel to her, and how much the death of her father is a sorrow shared by all.

The music helps to melt hearts; the food is excellent, the conversations begin superficially but slowly as the night approaches, become ever more intimate.

The daughter reports on the family in Rome but also recounts her nightmares with the Italian bureaucracy for which she was unprepared, entire days spent in endless queues or, accompanied by her uncle Caronte, negotiating the maze of Kafkaesque offices in order to submit a claim for her father's pension. But she also talks about her more intensive practice of yoga and meditation; it's clear that they both help her to absorb the great loss. She has a new depth, one can read it on her face, the experience of the death of her father to whom as a child she was very attached, has affected her deeply. She's not only his material but also his spiritual heir, a difficult burden to carry for a young woman who has always been quite reserved but who is now in the frontline of having to make decisions, of taking on the role of protagonist. Her boyfriend doesn't leave her for a moment; her younger brother runs around her like a puppy, not really knowing what to say but obviously happy that she's returned.

The mother is constantly on the move. She brings out hot dishes from the kitchen, takes the dirty ones back. She listens to conversations and intervenes briefly as she passes from table to table, fearful of moments of silence. She is hoping that her daughter may be pleased to be back in Sydney, that she'll be up to completing her university studies, that her boyfriend may be able to help her to revive her spirits.

The evening ends early; the flight from Italy is always tiring, emotions are high. The friends suggest meeting up again in the following days and, discreetly, leave.

*

The woman finds it hard to penetrate the ineluctable wall of suffering that her daughter puts up around herself after her return from Italy, and in which the mother imagines there may be an implicit rebuke of her separation from the father when the daughter was still so young. She always feels very inadequate and clumsy in her continual but failed attempts to open a channel of communication. Sensing the meaningful silence of her daughter, she becomes a bit silly, talking a lot, proposing lots of future projects. She continues to hope in a possible reconciliation but often, when alone, she despairs at how difficult it may be. She finds it hard to know what to do; she is unprepared, a mother who unfortunately is not up to the task.

She is happy that the boyfriend is living at Busby and hopes that her daughter is confiding in him when they shut themselves up for hours in the large upstairs bedroom.

On a loose slip of paper inside the wonderful *The Birth of Philosophy* by Giorgio Colli, which Giacomo had loved so much and which she has just begun reading again, one morning at dawn she scribbles:

"And so she now has two dead husbands".

The statement fills her with dismay. She has the feeling that she is connected with these two deaths, being almost, somehow, responsible for them.

It's as if, even as she enunciates it, the sentence decrees her guilt.

There is something in me that caused their death. Or, perhaps, it was me that made them die.

One was not enough, now another one as well.

This addition of "another one" chills her to the bone.

At other times, however, she feels like the victim of a cruel plot, of a universal conspiracy aimed to strike her down. Why her, in particular?

She looks around – relatives, friends, acquaintances – and finds no one with such a double tragedy behind them. There must certainly be even worse stories in the world than hers, she knows, but right now she feels like the only one and very alone.

One morning at dawn, sleepless and flustered as never before, she goes to Bronte Park. On a path overgrown with wild violets she crouches down to closely observe a file of busy ants. She is struck by the thought that, had she not stopped by chance, she would have surely trampled on a part of them.

She feels like she belongs to the part that would have been on the wrong side of chance.

The image of the Cosmic Chaos helps her to accept the painful events that have happened.

A short time later on a slip of paper used as a bookmark she writes: "Two days ago, I had a session with Kitty who read my aura.

She told me something absolutely unexpected that left me stunned: in spite of everything, she sees me as more open and freer, for the first time in a long time. As I came home, walking along Chesterfield Parade, shaded from the summer heat, I realised that she meant open and freer with respect to a possible romantic relationship. I've hit rock bottom. Perhaps there's a way up?

This seems to me to be a central node in my Busby saga.

The fog is beginning to clear."

*

She is still living in the downstairs room when she meets Warren for the first time.

She goes to a singles party. She has never gone to one before, but it's in Bondi at the house of Enea, a really nice male friend so she decides to go. Her black leather American aviator jacket bought from Michele, the second-hand clothes dealer in Rome behind Piazza Navona many years earlier, is reassuring, cool and warm at the same time. It's the beginning of spring in Sydney; the weather, as usual, is unpredictable.

Warren, whom she had not met before, at one point came into the room where people were dancing and she immediately noticed him on account of that amazing and magnetic blue aura of his, which intrigued her and led her to ask him who he is and where he comes from.

She discovers in the course of the conversation that he is from London, from an aristocratic family, with a degree in history from Cambridge. He has arrived the day before from the north-western desert of New South Wales where he had been on his own for six months, fossicking for opals. He had found quite a few and he now plans to sell them to finance his trip, first to India and then to England.

The woman, who has always had a fear of being alone and has only recently begun to come to terms with it, is struck with admiration for this character so outside the square. She accompanies him home – he's staying in Bondi with some friends – and they promise to see each other again. But nothing happens for several months.

They meet again at Paula's house, again in Bondi, at a party at the beginning of summer.

A gargantuan party: big house, big garden, people of all sorts. Really, all. Warren too. Who, this time, after an intense conversation about the state of the cosmos, asks her to meet him the next day in the late afternoon at Bondi Beach.

A long walk along the beach, their conversation ranges widely, crosses borders, recapitulates, pauses, takes off again. Like the wind that is now blowing and whipping up the waves. The woman is happy.

Warren walks her home. On top of the cliff they lie down on some grass, hidden by a sandstone boulder. There's a full moon. They kiss.

The next day they meet again at Busby. The house is deserted, the son is at a friend's, the daughter out with her boyfriend. It's a sign of destiny.

The room downstairs, her beautiful room, has a touch of magic in the moonlit evening, the lacy outlines of the three windows are projected on the bed where they make love.

And so begins their short-term relationship because Warren must leave in a few months; she knows there is no future for them, but this in a way reassures her. She feels that this relationship with Warren is a transitory affair, a crossing over from the loneliness of her years of mourning to the years of her inner renewal. She is thus forced to live in the present without illusions, above all without expectations, without a fairy-tale ending. That was what she had dreamed of as a teenager, encouraged from within her own family by the beautiful love story of her mother and father. It was what she had then hoped for in her long-term relationships, her two marriages which, right now, seem to her broken dreams, which shouldn't be repeated.

*

June, late in the evening, under the sign of Gemini.

After three years living in Sydney, the woman decides to organise a big party in honour of her zodiacal sign, the Gemini.

Birthday parties are recurrent events at Busby, as they had been in the family home in Rome. The long walnut table in her parents' dining room was, as she recalled, always crowded. Relatives, a variety of friends, colleagues of her father, new acquaintances, acquaintances of limited means, all took enthusiastic turns at the table. People ate, commented on the food, discussed politics, religion, quarrelled and then made peace, always around the dinner table, with everyone always happy to be together. When there was a special occasion to be celebrated, and that was a frequent occurrence, the table would be moved against the wall and all around there would be a great to-do, with all the guests inspecting, choosing and tasting the delicacies prepared just for them. The parties were opportunities for her mother, Maria, to exercise all her culinary creativity and the dishes, both the traditional ones and those from newly created recipes, were always prepared with enthusiasm.

It's for this reason that the woman relaxes instead of stressing when she organises a party of her own. It is a way of continuing the family tradition.

In Canberra, in the lovely house in Hovea Street, she had begun again, little by little, to invite at first only a few colleagues and then also friends of colleagues, students and former students. She was very fond of that house immersed in so much greenery, with its large bay windows in the living and the dining rooms, and, outside, the Roman pines to the left and, facing the entrance, tropical palms mixed with giant rhododendrons which reminded her of the Dolomites, even if up there in the mountains the flowers were tiny.

In Sydney she knows a lot more people so, shortly after returning from Canberra, any excuse is good to begin organising parties again. There are the birthday parties of the residents of the castle, parties of the former residents who now don't have a house large enough to have a big party, parties to celebrate specific events such as the arrival and departure of a house guest, a graduation, a new job, the departure for or the return from a trip, a wedding, parties for individuals, and group parties. The best parties however, those that are most talked about for time to come as parties that everyone remembers, are the themed parties.

Conceived and organised by the female family friend and by the daughter when they both lived at Busby while the woman was in Canberra, these parties mostly followed the astrological signs. The small veranda, easy to decorate with items bought at Recycled Garbage in Marrickville, visually portrayed the theme of the party.

With *La Dolce Vita*, the castle had been transformed into the set of Fellini's film, each room a scene from the film; even the laundry had been decorated. Fleeing Canberra, the woman had arrived late; in a silver-blue woollen sheath dress 1960s style and big dark sunglasses, she felt a bit like Anouk Aimée. For the festival of Pisces, the veranda, decorated in aquamarine bubble wrap, including the ceiling, had looked like an aquarium with waves and sea creatures on the walls, clothes and food all matching. Given their success, the parties had continued with one dedicated to Taurus, the Bull, the dominant colour being a fiery red, expressed in a lot of food with tomato sauce, beetroot, and meat cooked extremely rare.

Now it's her turn to organise the Gemini party.

Just to complicate things, in addition to the zodiacal theme, and in keeping with the duality inherent in her sign, she has decided to also include the theme of poetry, her great passion. Whoever among the guests feels in the mood, may climb onto the chest in the kitchen and recite a poem, either their own or by a favourite poet. Many try their hand; some acknowledged and very fine poets, some improvised poets, poets who recite in Italian, in English, in Lebanese, in Greek, even singers with their poems set to music. And to top it all, in the windowless alcove the woman places a projector with all her most abstract and most poetic slides rotating non-stop and breaking up over the dancers.

The woman is pleased; the evening has gone well even if a sense of melancholy has accompanied her at various times during the day and now grips her again as she says goodbye to the last guests and turns off the lights with the dawn coming on. She knows she'll have to drive Warren to the airport the next day. He is leaving for India to then go on to England. Their relationship is over and this party is their farewell. A farewell that she had foreseen but, in the event, finds difficult.

*

Deciding to move into the large bedroom upstairs is a major achievement for the woman and she does it only because her daughter and her boyfriend decide to leave the family home and go to live in a tiny apartment overlooking Bronte Beach. Now she comes to experience every separation, every departure, as an abandonment. It wasn't like that before. Before the annus horribilis it was she who wanted to leave, always wanting to get away. She saw life as an adventure, change as a means to curb her inner restlessness. But the daughter and her boyfriend need their independence, they must try to reconnect after their separation, after the death of the girl's father. The woman understands this even if she feels a little sorry.

The large room is very bright and north-facing, so that in the morning a warm and dazzling light enters through the windows and the thin damask turquoise curtains. In the space between the inside and the outside, wasps buzz freely. She likes lounging in bed in front of the windows when she can, which means rarely, but she likes it very much.

Her bed now is the one she brought from Rome, made by two traditional craftsmen working out of via Giulia.

In truth, the bed is a double-size sofa with its two raised sides. She had had one of the side rests removed as soon as she returned from Canberra by a very talented young Italian-Australian upholsterer. Giacomo had always been critical of that bed which he considered too short for him so now, even if, alas, only belatedly, she has also taken off the second side; finally it has become more open, more spacious. On the left, as soon as one enters the room, there is nonna Vittoria's chest of drawers, a late eighteenth-century French Empire piece. It had been restored in Rome before their departure for Australia by friends of an architect they had met in Algeria in the two years that Giacomo had worked there for Alitalia, and the woman had come and gone from Rome, sometimes with the little girl, sometimes alone. The architect's friends had done a good job restoring the chest of drawers, although they had asked for a lot of money for the restoration.

But at that time they, and especially the woman, didn't worry about expenses. They had enough money because of his job and there was also her tiny apartment in Trastevere which they would have been able to rent out at a good price. So instead of making a fuss and contesting the exorbitant figure, they had taken the hit and paid up. They felt lucky compared to many others of their generation; they were leaving, a great adventure awaited them, and so they could afford to be generous, they could squander. Between the two windows of the wall facing the door there's the small English George V table, which in viale Pinturicchio had stood in the entrance hall, supporting two candelabra, mostly for its aesthetic effect. Here, however, it will serve as her writing desk. It is made of cherry wood inlaid with ebony and was originally a sort of trolley without wheels to be placed in the middle of the hall because, with carvings on both its long sides, its short sides had two winglets that could be raised when necessary. On the right, apart from the bed that is on the same wall as the door, there is an open wardrobe, put up in a great hurry by the working bee of friends before Giacomo arrived from Mona Vale Hospital, in an effort to transform the house which, when it had been bought, appeared to have been abandoned for centuries, into an even minimally-adequate dwelling for a person who was seriously ill. The wardrobe should have had doors because it was very large and all the clothes, all the objects and the books heaped up there created a lot of confusion, especially in the often very confused mind of the woman. But at the time she didn't have a penny left so she had to leave it without doors. Now the wardrobe is still in the same condition, but the woman has created a sort of order among her things displayed there in plain sight; perhaps the order is imaginary but she nevertheless feels that she has more control now over the things around her and this makes her feel better.

The room with the pink walls had felt cramped when she lived there, but it had an ample view of the outside. The eye didn't linger on the inside, the scuffed and worn interior which, overall, created a rather romantic bohemian atmosphere but, with only the sloping ceiling that often leaked and the lopsided windows with the glass rendered opaque by time, provided very little to look at, indeed nothing worth the effort. The view outside, however, was magnificent: the sky, the sea, and the two bays and their outlines redeemed the poor interior. The large bedroom on the other hand is beautiful precisely on the inside. First of all, the inner stone walls give a special depth to the space and the air smells archaic, like the air she would breathe in the churches in Rome when she used to go there as a child, and later as an adolescent, and eventually no longer. A pity!

Now she dearly misses those churches and their smell. And she finds it again only in the Australian bush, in secret corners perhaps not visited for centuries upon centuries; there is the same smell there, the same sense of the sacred, of the return to origins that so fascinates and captivates her.

In this large bedroom she feels as though she is at the helm of Busby. From here she can direct all the operations that take place upstairs and downstairs. The windows look out over the front garden and thus, also over everyone who arrives, be it on foot, by bike or by car. She can also see her young son, now approaching adolescence, playing soccer in the street with Sean, his little blond friend who lives on the corner. The door of her room then opens out on a small entrance area, and from there onto the stairs. When the door is open, the voices from the other bedrooms and from the downstairs living room and the kitchen clearly resound; she can hear everything with the door open. The children, the friends, the cats, the guests (transient and semi-permanent), even the friends who knock on the door in search of comfort, who bring news, and cakes to have with coffee: Busby is a ship that gathers marooned souls from everywhere, and she is at its helm. At least that's how she feels in this moment.

*

There is only one fly in the ointment at this time.

She's employed at the University of Sydney on an annual contract, a precarious position that worries her for the first time in her life. She feels exposed, naked, on the other side of the world from where she could certainly live in more comfortable conditions, at least protected by the affection of family members and by the still large circle of friends and acquaintances.

She attempts to mentally retrace the path which, by force of circumstance, has seen her over time

- travel in luxury, first with Giacomo and Alitalia to Kenya, to the USA, to Algeria, then to Australia, one of the many places where they thought they would only remain for a year or two

- be an academic in Canberra, as the permanent member of a large international research university

- be safeguarded, therefore, in both instances by two major institutions, both times with a beautiful house, money and prestige

- finally finding herself here, a single woman with two children, little money, a fair number of debts, on fixed-term contracts, and an old manor house in ruins.

With her return to Sydney, her horizon is no longer brilliantly international.

She has lost status; she has come down from the brightly lit stairway. Money and economic security have never been a priority for her, but now they are a necessity.

She looks around, she hears the accounts of the early migrants, spends time with the more recent ones, listens to the arguments of her students, often of Italian-Australian origin, speaks above all with women, first- and second-generation migrants and realises – she always knew it but now she feels it in her bones – that to be a migrant is very different from being an expatriate. She feels out of place. Her former points of reference no longer serve to orient her in this land Down Under; her recently acquired ones are still very unstable. She feels she is standing on quicksand.

The emotional turmoil in her continues until she has an idea that she thinks may be able to help her.

She has met two outstanding women with whom she decides to explore, with curiosity and without prejudice, how the stories of Italian women who arrived in Australia some time ago and those who have arrived recently, relate to each other on important matters such as identity in a new land, a second language, art, ecology, culture, spirituality, health, politics, and the power of women in Italy and Australia.

They will organise a conference on the topic, a conference in order to understand, and to understand each other, a conference that will eventually be titled "The Italian-Australian Woman: Mapping an Identity". There will be 12 workshops over two days, at the end of which written reports will be drafted to be disseminated among the Italian community. SBS Radio will broadcast live interviews during the conference; in a dark corner a camera will be able to welcome women who want to tell their story "in secret".

The conference will be, at least for her, a profound experience but, she is sure, for the co-conveners as well. She is a fully born-and-bred Italian, Vanessa is second-generation Italian-Australian, and Joan, who works at SBS, is an Anglo-Australian married to an Italian. On nonna

Vittoria's table, pages and pages pile up as, little by little, the project takes shape.

>(VOICES OFF)
>
>... that the women of the first generation had had a hard time, very hard when they first arrived because they had not been the ones to make the decision to come to Australia, but had had to follow their husbands, that they had married by proxy and had for a long time been like ghost wives, that they had been single wives with dependent children; expectant girlfriends, who now regretted leaving their tiny village, missing the dialect, the relationships with other women of the family, the neighbours with whom they exchanged comments on everyday life; now feeling alone in a very distant and arid land so different from theirs, having to take care of the house and children and the colours and scents of their country of origin confined to their suburban gardens, with their husbands always worried about working as hard as they could with only a few words for their wives and children when they returned dead tired in the evening from the factory, who in Sydney after a few years had a more comfortable and larger house, in Leichhardt, in Five Dock, or in Haberfield, but with all those "fenze" here and there, a language they didn't understand, the strange habits, especially the food which was so different, that they felt alone and lost in the new continent that they couldn't manage to love and where it had taken such a long time to make some friends and only with people of their own hometown, from their region, people who spoke their

dialect and who reminded them a little of the life they lived in that place for which they were so homesick...

... that instead the women who had migrated recently had themselves chosen to come to Australia, a virgin land to be discovered alone or in company, for study, work or adventure, because they wanted a change in their life and had treated it like a nice vacation, then they had become engaged or separated, that they had found a good job, they had changed jobs from what they had done in Italy, they had travelled far and wide across the continent, they had studied or started new studies, they had felt at home in this new place, that they had felt free from the shackles of a restricted female life, from a religion that, even if no longer practised, did weigh on society and oppressed women who were interested in exploring new and exotic spiritual interests, who found a more liberated female condition Down Under, where women had begun voting in the early 1900s and this could be felt, really felt, and inspired trust and hope for a better life...

*

There had been a lot of enthusiasm for the conference.

Her female students from Sydney University had given her a hand, expert and generous friends had led the workshops, her daughter also had led a workshop on the relationship between the land of immigration and the land of origin. The daughter's boyfriend had taken care of decking out the location with giant black and white posters of Italian women and a pianist had played during the lunch prepared by Italian women of the first generation consisting of *fettuccine, gnocchi,* and *cavatelli* made by hand on the spot.

In her bedroom, from where this project had taken off, it now seems to her that her horizon may be widening again; that finally, her life may be opening up to new possibilities and not just entangled in the past. There is more clarity.

A *Vita Nova* again for her.

Consequently, it doesn't seem strange to her when, some time after the affair with Warren is over, at dusk on the bus to Canberra to visit her friends at the Australian National University, she has a fulminating encounter.

Albert is a young photographer with the Murdoch newspaper chain. She immediately tells him that she wouldn't be caught dead reading those newspapers. He smiles and agrees. They are sitting close together, the son, sitting in the window seat, is already asleep. When she gets up to go to the bathroom, she trips over Albert's leg and feels a current running through her from head to toe. In the three hours of the trip they recount their lives to each other. She can tell he is a good photographer; he is very curious and knows how to ask the essential questions, even the last and crucial one about her age. There are 15 years difference between them; she immediately thinks "not going there". He asks for her phone number; she gives it to him but adds yes, of course, just for a coffee.

In Canberra, they are slightly emotional when they say their goodbyes.

He is about to go spend a month in the bush in the mountains under the snow without a tent. He has travelled a lot, a French ex-wife, had worked as a model in Paris and then gone to Brazil, rafted down the Amazon River, speaks Portuguese. Now caught up in an irreconcilable quarrel with his latest pregnant ex, a jazz singer who wants to manage her pregnancy alone and exclude him completely. Traumatised by the idea of becoming a father without wanting to and without being able to decide anything, he thinks that a strong immersion in nature will help him understand and accept.

Back in Sydney, she thinks no more about it. It was a moment on the bus, a pleasant encounter, that's all.

One day her daughter tells her that a certain Albert (Albert who?) has left his number. She remembers and phones him back, always with the idea of sharing a coffee.

They meet up. In Bronte Park. He's on a bike, something of a professional rider; she now has short hair. He wants to see her again; she equivocates.

He phones her again at the university a few days later and tells her that he's bought a book for her and wants to give it to her. She's touched by this. Books are her passion, her weakness, her great friends since childhood; they represent creativity, dreams, escapism, her lullaby before falling asleep in the evening.

She agrees to visit him at his home in Erskineville.

They go out to eat at an Indian restaurant nearby. She hardly touches the food but talks a lot. She is still confused and flustered when they return to his home, a nice two-story federation terrace that he shares with two friends. He embraces her. She feels attracted but doesn't want to start an impossible relationship. He suggests a bath together in his antique tub with lion's paws. Albert has a way of doing things that undoes her; she feels his strong energy, she understands that he wants her and that he will have her. He is a Sagittarian full of fire and determination and a fantastic lover, she notices immediately.

So begins their relationship. They meet in Erskineville when she's free from her maternal commitments, in Busby when she's not.

It's a passion. There's no other way to explain the feeling between them since their meeting on the bus to Canberra. She feels completely desired, body and soul. Finally, after such a long time. And at the same time, she desires him with an intensity that she thought had been buried with Giacomo. She has always perceived her relationship with a man as a vehicle for her most profound expression which, at times, comes to be blocked at the surface. They read D.H. Lawrence together and *Lady Chatterley's Lover* is their favourite book.

In everything else, they couldn't be more different. Age, language, culture, temperament, way of life; yet the differences sharpen interest and respect. She likes everything about him, above all his sense of humour.

He's of Scottish origin and personifies the stereotype of the penny-saver; in other times she would have considered him a miser but in his case she feels tenderness for his attention to saving money, energy and food. Ecology is part of his political vision and she likes this a lot. Albert has a piece of land near Jervis Bay, on the south coast in the bush very close to the sea. They go camping there; after a day or two of walking barefoot among the snakes, she is no longer even afraid of them. One day they get lost in a clearing of old-growth trees, around them total silence. She feels it's a magical place, no one has ever been there before, she likes to imagine. They sit in each other's arms, without words, only looking with their eyes, feeling with their hearts.

Suddenly a lyrebird begins to sing. This is the Earthly Paradise, thinks the woman.

*

Busby during this period is no longer the central focus of her life. She certainly lives there and does everything she has to do: shopping, preparing lunches, dinners, especially for her son who is now consumed by his love of soccer. He sees and hears nothing else, he wants to become a champion and trains obsessively.

She is worried about school which holds no interest for him; sometimes they have terrible fights, she realises that she is losing control and doesn't know how to keep the situation in hand.

She alternates moments of great tenderness for her son with moments when she curses football and would like to set him some limits but there is nothing to be done. She's unable do it, he always wins. His desire for soccer is greater, more powerful, than his mother's desire to have him study. After all, she sees them at the university, the students who arrive from high school, some with very high grades from their final exams but who manage to achieve nothing and others who haven't achieved anything before, who are now ready to concentrate and to quickly graduate. So she never knows which is the right path towards which to steer the son. And perhaps she should just let him have his way.

Albert comes to Busby from time to time. He likes the castle very much. She always prepares special dishes for him; her son walks around him and watches him sideways as he plays football with his friend, Sean.

The daughter is pleased to see her mother happy. She now lives in Bronte Beach with her boyfriend but she always asks about her mother's love affair. The woman navigates her way between university, Busby, Erskineville, the conference on the Italian-Australian Woman, yoga three times a week, giving a few private lessons, and some social life.

Busby is now the place of duty, Erskineville the place of pleasure.

*

Late night, dining table, living room in a mess.

The mother, the daughter and the daughter's boyfriend are in feverish consultation. They are writing notices that they will put up around the castle the next day: there is to be a big party for the soon-to-begin renovations at Busby.

The money from the family inheritance has finally arrived and the woman has decided – with much hesitation but she has decided – to resume the project they had made immediately after purchasing the castle and then, by necessity, abandoned.

In a certain sense she now feels very Australian. Deciding to spend the inherited money and also take out a substantial mortgage while having only a temporary job is something she probably would never have done in Italy.

But here, in this land crossed for centuries by the Indigenous people with their light step, and where the whites have been pioneers accustomed to pick up and leave at the drop of a hat, the woman has more courage and is able to dare.

They have decided – the mother, the daughter and the boyfriend – to have some fun and amuse the guests, to rewrite the story of Busby halfway between reality and imagination.

It will be called "The Legend of Busby" and will be the fable of an ancient manor house where the family had arrived ten years earlier, lugging heavy weights on their shoulders.

The three authors are amazed at being able to remember and list all that has taken place there between those walls:

- the slow overwintering of bereavement

- the opening in stages to the outside

- a plate of pasta for visitors needing consolation

- the ever more numerous arrivals of relatives, friends, acquaintances staying at least overnight on the famous green sofa in front of the TV or in some bedroom for a few days, a week, a month.

Busby is described as a "not-for-profit community welcome centre" where a bancha tea, yoga lessons, soccer coaching, shiatsu massage, and endless friendly counselling are available from the generous inhabitants.

Invited guests will be asked to participate, to add to or modify the historical reconstruction with personal comments, and memories either in writing or recorded on video during the party.

With furious haste, the boyfriend dictates, the daughter suggests changes and writes. Placards with drawings and coloured images pile up on the floor. Many, many bouts of laughter. It will be a party to remember, one hopes.

The woman is pleased. She imagines a better future. She imagines the upcoming works may be able to sweep away that residue of sadness, nostalgia and suffering that has held sway there for so long. She hopes that the demolition of walls and the installation of no less than 10 windows may provide new light, new air to the environment, and attract and generate more positive energies. Having completed their work, smiling, they make a toast. A new era opens up for Busby.

*

Evening following the party.

In the windowless alcove the television is on, bodies are piled up on the sofa, on the cushions, on the floor. Leftovers of the legendary food of the night before are on offer in the kitchen where chaos reigns; nothing has yet been put away, everyone is exhausted, all the cleaning up will be done tomorrow. On the screen appear the interviews conducted the night before by the daughter's boyfriend, now a seasoned documentary filmmaker. The talking heads of the guests, filmed now standing now sitting, the faces sometimes in full close up, the music and noise in the background all bring back the joyous atmosphere of the party and a bit of emotion can be felt in the air. An era is over.

Busby will undergo a multiple surgical operation. The prospect of change, as often happens, generates enthusiasm but also loss, even a little anxiety. Everyone is pleased with how the party went, everyone has their own personal story of Busby to tell, everyone hopes that the renovations will not disperse all that collective energy that they have so loved. The woman watches herself speaking, smiling and laughing on the screen. The long and tight Dotti blue evening dress highlights the shape of her thin body. Her hands, her arms wave in the air and make the aluminium bracelets rattle. They remind her of Lamu and the wonderful journey on a sailboat that she and Giacomo had taken at the end of the last year spent in Kenya, immersing themselves in the exotic: the Milimani Hotel in Nairobi where they lived for a year; Mombasa and mosquito nets; safaris in the national parks; the dreams written down every morning at dawn; the Europeans like pale puppets only with heads; the vibrant bodies of the Africans. Close up, the woman looks lithe, and very young. Or perhaps it's the joints she's smoked that give her that air. She makes a few ironic remarks about herself: about Busby, about life there with her children, about the tragic events she has suffered as if she hadn't been scarred by them. It's clear that she's pleased with the success of the party and the affection of the many friends who came. She seems to lack much depth. In their interviews, both her children seem more serious, more profound and aware of the heavy history that they leave behind. They don't criticise the mother. Perhaps they accept her as she is. Her dear friend Nica is always telling her that she's like a reed in the wind.

THE DAY OF THE BEGINNING

The front door is thrown open and allows the builder and two born-and-bred Greek workmen to come through. The renovation of Busby after ten long years, after all that has happened there to its inhabitants, is finally beginning.

They're all waiting for Amit, the architect who's a fan of Glenn Murcutt and his open verandas. The woman finds herself in perfect accord with his architectural approach. It's a challenge and a pleasure to discover all the wonderful things that could be tried out at Busby. The woman's father, himself an engineer, had wanted her to study architecture; instead she had chosen literary studies although years later, returning to Rome from New York, she had taken up urban photography, photographing interiors and architectural exhibitions. In the end, her father's suggestion had resonated with her. She now throws herself into the renovation project with great enthusiasm.

A baptistery was how Amit had immediately defined the castle, when she and Giacomo had approached him about renovating it, years before, shortly before Giacomo's illness.

Amit had come up with an ambitious project and she had immediately fallen in love with it; they weren't worried about money at that time and wanted to complete it as soon as possible. Instead, after Giacomo's death, she had found herself obliged to take photos of houses designed by Amit to pay him for the work he had already done for them.

Many years had passed since then, and now would seem to be the right time. The project is more modest, costs have risen during these ten years and she is certainly no longer the person she used to be. But, even with its slight modifications, she likes the design a lot. Amit finally arrives. Everyone is standing to attention. He smiles at her with those liquid light blue eyes that easily become teary when he's emotional. He immediately begins to give instructions in a voice that is velvety and deep and which touches her profoundly.

The work will begin in the bathroom and kitchen. Then it will stop while the entire rear section which has been added to the original building will be demolished, including the first floor, the ground floor and the laundry below. All appear to contain asbestos and so all need to be replaced.

The woman prepares some strong coffee, serving it in small cups; Greeks, Jews, Italians, they all prefer it that way. Then it begins.

The first blow of the pickaxe is for her a blow to the heart. A part of her history is going, memories crowd in, all that could have been and was never realised. A big change. Has she made the right decision? Suddenly she doesn't feel so sure.

Amit smiles at her again; he's enthusiastic about the project and he communicates it to her, so she relaxes, feels that he can be trusted. It will all go well.

*

There are no parties at Busby during the two very long years of the renovation.

Friends frequently drop by but never in groups, because in the downstairs room now used as a living room, beside the piles of books, there's only room for one or two people to sit at the table. They stop by for a coffee, a chat and sometimes a pasta. The curious neighbours can't stop checking it out. Cosmo, the cat, has decided for now to go and live in the house across the street; too many changes stress him and the couple across the road adore him. Every now and then he returns to the ancestral castle, briefly licks Coco, who misses him a lot and then, with a sigh, goes off. When will all this confusion end, he asks himself.

After the first three hectic months in which the bathroom is renovated and a kitchen is created in the alcove, now furnished with a wonderful spacious window that will bring light to that former dark cavern so loved by the family and its entourage, life at Busby flows slowly for the woman and for her son. For several months nothing happens. After some time it becomes clear that the builder has accepted a major job in Campbelltown. It involves the construction of multiple townhouses and thus a lot of money to be made, so the castle is abandoned by the workmen and the woman and her son remain buried in the dust and debris in a wait that seems endless. The beds upstairs now also serve as sofas for reading, listening to music, resting during the day and hosting close friends with whom to conduct long conversations without being disturbed. As for her relationship with Albert, after a dramatic period of separation due to the unexpected arrival of his other ex, this time the Brazilian woman, it is passionately resumed right there in the Roman bed that the woman has dragged around the world. He is very determined in his desire to rent a house with her and her son. A house that isn't Busby, with everything that has happened to her there. They could begin a new life, the three of them. The woman is unable to decide. It's taken a long time to get the works approved. Now that they have begun and will sooner or later finish, she would like to enjoy the renovated castle. And in any case she wouldn't want yet another new home for her son at this point, after all the changes he has already had in his young life. She made this mistake with her daughter, dragging her from one continent to another; she doesn't want to repeat herself. She also senses that a relationship with a man several years younger, with him, with Albert, would be difficult to carry on for a long time; better to live it in the present without committing too much to the future. For the first time in her life she doesn't feel the anxiety of a possible abandonment; for the first time *carpe diem* becomes her daily mantra.

*

Dawn of the year 2000, the new millennium, the large bedroom.

Sleepy, stupefied and very happy, the woman slips down under the sheets and sees again, as if in a trance, images of the previous 24 hours, images that pile up endlessly and will remain, she thinks, in her memory forever:

- Chowder Bay where she spent the day of New Year's Eve with her son, her friends, Robbie and Sonja, their children and Robbie's brother and his wife who have come from Italy for the occasion

- the burning heat that welcomes them on arrival in the morning together with the hundreds of people already crowded everywhere, sleeping bags, multicoloured surfboards, chairs, even some armchairs, tables, little tables, large tables overflowing with food and drink of all kinds

- the frantic search for a shady place to spend the many hot hours yet to come

- the tangible air of anxious waiting, the sensation of feeling all united in the face of the epochal event (perhaps the end of the world?), certainly unique in the short life of each of those present

- the splendid bay, polished to perfection, with hundreds and hundreds of boats of all kinds from everywhere, with occupants who are already toasting, dancing, diving into the sea and greeting everyone with big smiles

- the deafening music that comes from a thousand different directions

- the expectancy that becomes spasmodic as the hours pass in the subtropical heat, the children showing signs of impatience after repeated swims and gargantuan meals

- and then the twilight, the sun that turns red in front of the astonished crowd which for a moment becomes silent; can it perhaps be their last sunset, the woman wonders, while the red light streaking across the bay seems to transport her into a science fiction film in which some extra-terrestrial being can suddenly appear (everything is possible on the eve of such a great event)

- the count down that begins around 11 in the evening and appears unending; the breeze that comes off the bay refreshing bodies and hearts; the music that becomes sweeter, people begin to hug one another, never-ending toasts, everyone loves everyone else, we're all together, it's all bigger than us, little ants in an immeasurable universe

- time, the greatest mystery of all, the present which is completely relative, the now which is an illusion, all this suddenly takes on an extraordinary importance

- Sydney time becomes the Time that everyone there around the bay – more than a million people – obsessively refer to, minute by minute, in spasmodic succession

- the bay that just before midnight becomes an immense stage invaded by lights of all colours, the famous giant Chinese lanterns swinging on the water while hypnotic music seems to direct them in a sort of circular ballet

- and then the fireworks, magnificent mad fireworks on the Harbour Bridge, the Opera House, Darling Harbour, connected, separated, sparkling, hypnotic, fireworks that never seem to end in this long, very long, midnight of the new millennium that finds us still alive and that gives us hope that everything will be well.

BUSBY RENOVATED

That the interior of the castle may have changed so radically could not have been imagined from the outside. The facade still had the same beautiful sandstone walls, the three-part window of the front downstairs room, shaded by the orange tree, by now grown and full of fruit, the two upstairs windows under siege from the usual wasp nest. Only the front door was different, made of opaque glass and rusty iron in a Gothic design by the architect which underscored the enchanted atmosphere at Busby. Magnificent. And as soon as one turned down the little path on the left, one would see no less than five brand new windows, two in the original stone wall and three in the extension that constituted the living room. Not only. Looking up to the top floor, one would notice three more windows, one added to the middle room and two to what had been the pink room. And then, at the back, facing south and therefore towards the sea, one would see the two large uncovered terraces on the first and second floors, whereas the former laundry, now a new one-room studio apartment, still overlooked the garden below but was now furnished with a lovely outdoor area.

The terraced garden, with its sandstone steps at the side, had assumed an exotic air for the Italic inhabitants, with the fern tree by now grown enormous, as had the very high palm, and the tufts of bird of paradise springing up colourfully all over the place.

The castle, during the two long years of its renovation, had been closely watched by curious neighbours who were also perhaps a little surprised that the new owners, who had arrived at Busby in such a parlous state, had managed to pull themselves back into shape and transform the dilapidated hovel into a beautiful and comfortable residence.

The castle now came to be described as a luminous beacon, a centre of attraction, a lodestone of energy for the inhabitants, friends, acquaintances, and even the curious passers-by. Photos were taken and films shot inside it; Busby had passed into history.

*

A colour photo, size 25 x 9 cm, wide-angle, 18mm.

In the foreground on the Frate glass table, partly covered by a light-coloured mat, three cakes with lighted candles. One cake with chocolate and cream, two of them topped with almonds, each with a red flower in the middle.

Immediately behind, her body bent over, cheeks puffed up and ready to blow out the tiny flames, the woman is in the centre, her two female friends on either side. A special moment.

The woman is dressed in an orange chiffon dress, tight-fitting and pleated on one side, with both hands holding back her hair close to her face in order to avoid it catching on fire. On her right Patty, dressed in black lace with her left hand resting lightly on the woman's shoulder; on her left Rosalyn, in a pink and silver top which she tightens with both hands behind her back. All around the table glasses of red wine, of white wine, of champagne, full bottles, empty bottles.

Standing behind them, a motley crowd crammed together. Smiling. One can tell that they're all waiting for the fateful moment to begin singing Happy Birthday. A female singer with a microphone in hand, perhaps on a small stage placed at an angle at the back of the large living room, leans forward in the distance above her friends in order to appear in the photo. She too is ready to sing. Much happiness.

On the left in the photo, through a large glass door one can see the brightly lit terrace and the tip of the fern tree coming up from the garden. On the right the two entrances cut into the sandstone wall lead into the kitchen with the marble table piled high with pots and plates. Behind the friends, above the sofa, in the distance, multicoloured posters exalting the Twins, the zodiacal sign that's being celebrated at the moment.

Birthday party and end of renovations; the castle is open again.

*

After two long years, mother and son can finally relax and begin to reorganise the rooms on the upper floors which, during the cyclopean works, have become dusty deposits of objects of all types and sizes, necessarily removed from the lower floors undergoing demolition.

Smell of paint, of floor wax, light, so much unusual and dazzling light that penetrates from the numerous new windows. A new energy.

And the comings and goings begin again.

The daughter and her boyfriend are almost daily guests; they live in Bronte Beach, a ten minutes' walk; morning or evening a meal together is always a celebration, a recounting to each other of how much the castle has changed for the better, every room, every corner, top, bottom, front, back. What a delight!

The teenage son can now invite his friends over; there is again space in his room which is even brighter. The mother had been keen to have another window opened in the stone wall; as a result of the greater light the room seems almost double the size. Blaring music; in the early morning or late evening, rap spills out into the street.

The cats are happy. Instead of having to go around the house to get to the back garden for food, they can now elegantly jump from the new large kitchen window down into the little lane at the side and from there reach their bowls. They can also, again from the said window, surveil their enemies, especially old Jerry and his starving and belligerent acolytes, even if Cosmo is no longer scared and brilliantly defends his territory, not to mention his beloved Coco. He has now become Busby Parade's local king-pin.

Dorian, the daughter's long-time friend, an actor, painter and now a jeweller's apprentice, rents the large room upstairs. In addition to sleeping in it, he will make it his atelier; he has many ideas and an indomitable artistic fury. Everyone knows that when he begins a project, he always manages to complete it successfully.

The tiny one-room studio apartment is rented to a young actress with little money who is looking to become famous. Smiling and chatty, all excuses are good for her to go upstairs; a cup of tea, some advice, a story, lots of laughs.

The new imposing Gothic door is now often open in the evening; it was time to begin to have visitors again! And many arrive in groups, to say hello, to have a look, to evaluate, go up and down stairs, in the front and the back, unending comments; the owners seem like estate agents. Very happy.

The Italian friends and relatives who followed the progress of the renovations from afar now get in line to make a pilgrimage to Sydney. Having seen the photos and heard the oral stories, they want to see the miraculous transformation in person.

*

It's early morning. Beginning of March, the air is hot and dry, perhaps a Monday.

The front door opens wide and lets the woman pass through; bag, books, loose papers in one hand, a bunch of keys in the other. Something falls from her to the ground: it's the jacket she had draped over one shoulder. She loses her patience, picks it up; it's clear she's in a hurry. She brushes past the rosemary hedge, the scent spreads into the surrounding air, she breathes it in. She smiles.

She gets into the car, waits a minute or two, then begins sounding the horn.

After another five minutes the son runs out of the house and stumbles towards the car. The shirt of his uniform unbuttoned, tie on one shoulder, backpack on the other, shoes in hand. They're going to be late. He for school, she for university. They also need to go to Clovelly to pick up Ned, a fellow student, the son suddenly remembers. The mother becomes furious.

The journey to the International Grammar School in Ultimo is made in silence by the mother; a lot of chatter in the back seat.

The two teenagers talk about video games, about the latest action film they've seen, about girls, few of the ones at their school are worthy of any attention in their view, the best are always those one meets outside, at parties or at the beach.

While driving, the mother concentrates on the lesson she has to deliver in the afternoon and above all on the schedule of the radio program that she is finally conducting at Rete Italia for students taking courses in Italian as a second language. She needs to finish it before lunch. No trivial task: need to contact the female student who acts as her assistant and who goes around to schools and universities, recording small segments of theatrical pieces, songs, poems, stories that the students produce and which she and her colleague, Ciro, edit for the weekly broadcast; find the music to insert between the spoken sections and the guest of the week; record a nursery rhyme for the primary school children, one chosen by Pat, her colleague from Canberra; make sure that her former colleague Leo, a former commedia dell'arte actor, will recite a poem appropriate for university students during the program, phoning it in from a public telephone.

Suddenly the mother pricks up her ears: in the back the two teenagers are talking quietly but with great excitement about sex and, after having explored other possibilities in great detail, they reciprocally declare themselves to be heterosexual. She can't remember ever having this kind of conversation with her schoolmates, but, of course, times have changed and Sydney is the gay city par excellence so it has become second nature for adolescents to identify their own gender and sexual orientation. Moments of silence follow these declarations which are so intimate and so important for both of them. Then the chatter resumes: about computer games, Sport, football and tennis, about girls. The mother brakes; they have arrived at the school. The two rush out in a flash; they hope they aren't late again but the door seems to be shut, so for the umpteenth time they will have to report to the principal.

The woman heads towards Sydney University at full speed, risking a heavy fine; Service NSW is not as forgiving as the Italian traffic police can sometimes be; with the latter there's always the hope of getting away with it.

She and the son will meet again late in the afternoon in the castle, hungry and with lots of things to recount to each other.

The woman is already looking forward to the evening, lentil soup and steamed bok choy, football, and a new Martin Scorsese film to watch together, right mum? Then, up into her new bedroom, window wide open, the humming of crickets, the music of waves, and always the scent of honeysuckle.

*

The former pink room, now a very beautiful bright bedroom with a terrace opening onto the sea, is occupied, once the renovations have happened, by the mother who claims it brooking no challenge, but with none proffered by the children.

After more than a year spent with her son in captivity in the cloven castle, the woman now breathes a sigh of relief. And, with satisfaction, she mentally lists the changes that have occurred

- the tiny studio apartment in the back garden

- four bedrooms

- a huge living room

- a viable kitchen

- two bathrooms, two terraces

- all of it on three floors, with the gardens, both front and back, also rejuvenated.

It's been a long and complicated process but she's made it; she has kept her promise. It's too late for Giacomo but, ten years later, the house has become, finally, what they both had wanted it to be.

The woman indulges her whimsy in furnishing her new room, mixing antique and modern, nonna Vittoria's chest of drawers and a chaise longue as a bed; a minimalist wardrobe, exotic objects, souvenirs of other lives spent in Nairobi, in Algiers, in New York. Here now, fronting the sea, a distant view of Clovelly, Coogee, all the way to Malabar, a string of postcard beaches. She feels open after such a long time, liberated and pleased to have managed to complete this Herculean task.

The room is now accessed by a comfortable wooden stairway that leads to a small landing, microscopic but useful for creating a space of expectation and mystery. The architect has followed the tenets of Feng Shui which advise against having a direct line from the front door of a dwelling to the window or balcony. He believes that positive energies dissipate in this way and so favours an entrance from the side. Amit, who is a Hungarian Jew interested in Hinduism and in the meditation practised on the mountain peaks of Tibet, thinks it best to try to satisfy all the different types of possible clients, including Chinese people, in case she may want to sell the property. The woman, wanting to ensure the good energy of the house, has had Feng Shui readings done of the castle, both before the beginning and after the completion of the renovations. Apparently Busby, at the time they had bought it, had been a disaster but now, with the light flooding in from many new windows and with the water fountain always flowing in the front downstairs room, the Chi should improve and the woman already feels that it has.

In the morning, after opening the French window of the former pink bedroom, the woman sits down, even if only for a few minutes, on the beautiful sunny terrace. She looks at the sea, there on the horizon, and takes a deep breath; she closes her eyes and allows herself to be kissed. She has always had a close relationship with the sun: it does her good, she feels it, it warms her up, gives her strength when she feels weak. Come to think of it, the ritual worship of the Sun god by the Ancients was nothing more than a way to feel in harmony with the true source of life. Are we not, all of us, as the scientists now maintain, stardust? And our own star is indeed the sun.

Little by little, since she arrived in Australia, it seems to her that her philosophical horizons have become wider, clearer, or, at the very least, more suited to her character. She feels that, like the universe, her own body exists in an equilibrium which is continually changing, with all the organs interacting, sometimes in harmony, sometimes in contrast. Since the mind and the emotions are strongly influenced by the well-being of the body, it's clear that the body must be healed in order to heal the psyche: *mens sana in corpore sano.*

Her resonance with Aboriginal Australian culture, with its stories of the sky and the earth being animated through dreams in an eternal present, make her rethink how she has lived her own story and the story of the generations that have preceded her. The past seen as the locus of transition, the imperfect tense; she, always in flight, always projected towards a better future. Now, her warm body stretched out on the deck chair, the sound of the sea in the distance: for a moment she understands that she did well to stay in Australia. Here, Down Under, now, without any reference point, she has been forced to start over, to experiment in the present, without having her back covered, without being able to lean on the past, here, in an unknown and very different place from where she had come.

It's taken a considerable effort which, somehow, seems to her to have opened up new horizons. Often she happens to doze off for a moment in the sun with a smile on her lips.

*

Christmas Eve, hot, humid, subtropical sunset.

In the brand-new living room with the

- blackbutt timber floor salvaged by a scavenger from a house being demolished in Rose Bay

- giant sliding glass door that opens all the way along the terrace with its tropical-blue railing

- sandstone walls brought back to their original state

- *A Moment of Mine on the 4th April 1928 at 10.02*, a print of Giacomo Balla's painting above the white sofa

- small art deco table bought in Newtown for $30 a year or so earlier

- large vase of tiger lilies with an exotic scent

many friends have gathered.

All spread out on the sofa, on chairs, cushions, carpets, latecomers also spilling out onto the terrace. Finally there's enough space. The warm air seems tender, the scent of honeysuckle is a mixture of honey and lemon.

This year there's something new at Busby; there's not only the Christmas Eve dinner.

At sunset all those present, passionately brought together, enjoy a communal moment of reflection with readings and speeches which may restore to Christmas some of its original meaning: the birth of a great prophet who preached the message of love for oneself and for others. The woman still nostalgically remembers the Christmas Eve dinners at her parents' home. Light dinners, always the usual menu: spaghetti with tuna, mixed fried fish and vegetables, sautéed broccoletti, orange and olive salad, dates, almonds and dried figs. Then the magic of midnight Mass, reached on foot with shoes creaking on the asphalt in the silence of the night, the intoxicating scent of incense in Santa Croce al Flaminio, the flowers, the songs, the candles. It's all still alive in that corner of her memory that the woman calls childhood; together with that image of her seen in so many black and white photos, a refined little girl with a large mass of dark hair and very black eyebrows. And a serious face, always a serious face.

The woman is now serene. And often smiling.

It came to her all of a sudden, this idea of transforming the usual overindulgence into a revisitation of the meaning of Christmas, the end of the year being so close making it the right time to rethink the meaning of life. She is pleased with the decision. Many friends have recently approached diverse "spiritual" practices. Here we're in the East, so, along with Vipassana meditation, Zen meditation, yoga nidra, tai chi, chi kung, rebirthing, and visualisation, all the guests are also open to talking about Jesus, seeing that it is his day of celebration. Or we could talk about what he evokes: peace, social justice, love, the need for some poetry in the world.

Some initial embarrassment – it *is* a novelty – then very slowly the atmosphere loosens up and everyone contributes a story, a poem, a song, that everyone listens to in silence. A communal feeling is created, a community different from the usual bedlam of loud debates charged by alcohol; one doesn't need to say a lot to feel close, a strong energy connects the whole group. A moment of silence, a pause at the end, before dinner. Now everyone can enjoy with gusto the spaghetti with tuna, chicory and broad bean dip, orange and olive salad, dried figs.

The castle is now magnificent and appealing not only to friends but also to strangers. The woman is proud of it.

*

The kitchen is a little jewel.

Replacing the dark and, in subtropical summers, very humid alcove, it now benefits from its eastern aspect to filter a pink morning light through the large window cut into the sandstone. The cats love it. From there, in one impressive leap, they often land on the fence that separates Busby from the property next door, a 1930s apartment building inhabited by a young and likeable couple with three daughters; he a Scottish Australian, she an Irish rover, who had found herself in Sydney by chance and then remained forever.

In front of the window a capacious sink, a child could use it as a bath. Here, finally, the woman can wash tons of fresh vegetables, which, when she has the time, she cooks in a variety of ways and which can then be utilised by the family during the week.

The round marble table, a table which she had had made by the neighbourhood marble worker living behind her house in Trastevere, in an old-style workshop handed down from father to son, now dominates next to the wall opposite the gas stove, no longer the antediluvian one which, with its leaks, often risked blowing up the house and its inhabitants. An Italian gas stove, of course. And here the woman begins to list with great enthusiasm all the delicacies that she can finally cook now, after years of enforced creative drought. Not only can the burners be adjusted to perfection when suddenly she needs to lower the heat and go from a quick searing to a long cooking time, but the oven, the oven is a marvel! It's electric and adjustable to the tiniest degree. The woman has fun preparing *lasagne*, fish with potatoes, macrobiotic apple pies without sugar, only raisins and almonds.

On the table, for special events, one can now prepare very light potato gnocchi, made without eggs and with little flour. There, too, sheets of dough can be rolled out to make white and green fettuccine, which are then laid out on the sofa wrapped in sheets dusted with flour. At the table, the woman now also improvises lessons for the daughter's friends who have a desire to immerse themselves in the grammar of Italian cuisine, picking up basic rules about garlic, oil and chilli, butter with onion, never cheese on pasta with clams, all rules that Australians often don't know but would like to learn by rote.

At last, a kitchen where the woman can experiment, at times recalling recipes from the past and with them those flavours, smells and atmospheres; nostalgia and novelty hand in hand. Opera always goes well with it all; Pavarotti and Callas are her favourites.

*

A Friday morning, 10 a.m.

In addition to the lunches, the dinners, the bancha teas, and the aperitifs with relatives-friends-acquaintances, all in the living room, all around the Frate table fully on display on the left, near the kitchen and in front of the two brand new windows, the woman thinks of organising private lessons in Italian language and culture in the gaps between her university classes. She has a sizeable mortgage to pay after the recent renovations and even though she has rented the largest bedroom to Dorian, a long-time friend of her daughter, what, with her still-dependant son, the bills and everything else, she can't afford to dawdle. The first group of students is very interesting. They come from the Centre for Continuing Education at Sydney Uni. All middle-aged, all highly educated, all multilingual, all very different from each other. There is a psychiatrist who is a former opera singer, an ex classical ballet dancer, a writer, an actress and director, a university professor of ancient Roman history, another former dancer, another history teacher, a journalist fluent in Spanish, in short, a rich mix of expertise and creativity. All are interested in continuing to learn about Italy, the language, the politics, the art, the literature, the food. All thirsting for new knowledge, they want to know simply everything. The woman finds herself at ease with them, she knows that she can offer them what also interests her in the various areas, so the exchange is reciprocal. They meet on Friday mornings for three hours, Italian coffee and biscuits supplied as part of the cultural ceremony. Little by little, thanks to a continuous word of mouth, the woman finds her diary full of afternoon appointments, lessons to groups, to couples, even single students; those who last the distance are always those with whom she feels some elective affinities. Her academic experience has given her the ability to use multiple teaching techniques and, furthermore, her innate curiosity renders the work interesting and allows her to maintain a continuous link with her motherland. A strong and necessary bond which somehow forces her – she has realised – to put her immersion in English on the back burner. She still has a strong Italian accent and a chronic insecurity due to not having studied English at university but having picked it up quickly and in tragic circumstances when left alone with two children. At times it seems to her that living in Australia allows her, rather than letting herself be permeated by the local language, to observe, savour, penetrate better from the outside, her native language. Not that she doesn't like English. Having, indeed, despised it in her adolescence – infatuated as she had been with the Parisian French of the existentialists and the *chansonniers* – she had then embraced it out of necessity in terra australis and subsequently come to really appreciate it. English has drawn out a part of herself that she would otherwise have allowed to lie dormant: that part that has forced her to face practical responsibilities, to speak and write using a language that isn't hers, a language acquired without rhetorical flourishes, returning words back to their original value and meaning. It has taught her the humility of having to begin to speak again in a simple way, almost childlike, instead of using big words as she had liked to do in illo tempore when she was at the university, in the public assemblies, in her fired-up political speeches. She understands that this consonantal language so different from her own, this language has indeed helped her to understand the coexistence of differences. There isn't a better or worse, there is only a difference that is neither better nor worse; there's only a combination in her of the before and the now. She feels like a hybrid.

And so the glass table, between breakfasts and dinners, fills up with sheets of paper, pens, books, notebooks, scribbled notes, underlined sentences, finger marks, leftover coffee, biscuits, forgotten bags, accumulated energies, daring experiments.

*

The bathroom is a marvel:
- the old timber floor brought back to light
- the Italian porcelain basin
- the triangular Jacuzzi under the shower
- the soft lights

Each morning the woman repeats to herself that she likes she likes she very much likes her new bathroom!

With Albert early on, when Busby had been cut in half and they had begun seeing each other again, the renovated bathroom had become the central part of their nightly ceremonies. Candles, scented oils, frangipani, hibiscus, alternated on the edges of the spa, while they lathered each other.

The bathroom had been their first meeting place in Erskineville; the first physical contact between them had been in the tub with the lion's feet, thereafter repeated over time as a ritual.

Even the last time that they had seen each other, the definitively last time, the bathroom had welcomed them. He had told her with tears in his eyes that perhaps, just perhaps, he wanted to try again with his Brazilian ex. The woman, however, as something of a challenge, had quoted him an aphorism by Friedrich Nietzsche, scribbled by who-knows-who on one of the placards for the party announcing the beginning of the renovations, which had then hung in plain sight in the corridor so that she could repeat it to herself every time she entered and left the castle: "Life is made up of extremely rare moments of great intensity and of innumerable intervals".

The last time, too, they had said their last things to each other in the Jacuzzi, with the water flowing along with the tears. For the first time, however, she felt ready to be abandoned; it had been a wonderful affair that had to end before turning into a nineteenth-century pulp melodrama.

So when they had come out of the bathroom, their hair as wet as their faces, they had lingered in the corridor in front of the sign bearing Nietzsche's aphorism, unable to decide what to do.

In the end she had been the one to decide. A hug, and a definitive goodbye.

*

Early afternoon, passing drizzle, sun breaking through the clouds.

There are five of them, all female friends.

In a circle, two on the small sofa, one on the large armchair on the side, one on the small round armchair, one on the floor with crossed legs; the front room with the triple window provides the right atmosphere for a meditation session.

Five friends, all Italian but very different in age, character, geographical origin and cultural background. A rich mix.

Silence, blessed precious silence, incense and candles in abundance. And then the stories.

About how the session has gone, about what it has drawn out from the conscious and unconscious, the emotions, the laughter, the tears and then life-stories that inevitably emerge from each one. Past and recent. Intimate stories. Happy stories, dramatic stories; stories, and more stories. Fascinating.

Having started with enthusiasm at the beginning of her Australian adventure, continued with new-found discipline for some time, then abandoned, resumed and abandoned again, meditation has for the woman been a thread, fragmented but still a thread, through her life in Australia. Having known and practised it gives her the security that she can always return to it if she wants, and she knows that it is good for her.

Once the affair with Albert is over, the woman realises that it is the right time to start again.

Indeed, it is necessary because after their farewell, she plummets into a period of abysmal uncertainty; she continually asks herself if her sudden decision to end it may not perhaps have been dictated by a stroke of pride. Did it really match her desire?

She was the one who put an end to their relationship. He had still been undecided. Even if it was clear, the woman sensed it, that he would have wanted to try again with his ex. But why did she end it so abruptly?

And is she, then, so sure of having done the right thing? The more time passes, the more she remembers her relationship with Albert as a series of wonderful colour slides, one romantic scene after another, erotic, poetic scenes, all wrapped up in the wild nature of the Australian bush. Everything beautiful, everything positive, everything perhaps still possible if she hadn't... if it hadn't been...

Sleepless nights.

Uncertain and conflicted, she sometimes thinks back to her last meeting with Albert with a critical eye. Her mind tells her that she did well, that the relationship with Albert could have gone on perhaps a little longer, but then? What future could it have had?

Instead, her heart and her often uncontrollable emotions whisper to her that she could have revealed to Albert her desire to be together despite everything, confess to him her not apparent but always present fragility and her fear of abandonment. Loneliness now frightens her.

Perhaps because since she was a child she had lived in a family with four men, father, brothers and a bachelor uncle. Romantic relationships are easy and bold in their initial phase, but they turn out to be more complex and contorted as little by little one arrives at the deepest of intimacies. There, there's a deep-seated lack and thus an irrepressible desire to feel herself loved, desired, possessed. A desire revealed in rare moments of perfect understanding, often hidden out of modesty or pride.

She often returns to the cliff which saw them walking arm in arm early in the morning before going to work or late at night, with the full moon rising from the sea or even in the dark, which is never completely so, one only needs to get used to it.

The teaching that she so loves, the maternal duties, the care of the house, the shopping, lunches, dinners to prepare, everything weighs on her at the moment. She would like a holiday, lying by the sea for hours, doing nothing.

She repeats to herself that it will pass, that time is the best medicine; she lives in one continuous seesaw of conflicting feelings.

Her female - and her male - friends, but above all her very sensitive female friends, are present, many conversations with tea and sweets, some outings, the cinema, parties, but finally the suggestion that draws her out of her torpor: a small group meeting once a week in the renovated castle. For the first time since her separation from Albert, the woman accepts with a surge of enthusiasm. She knows it will be an important routine in order to regain her mental balance. She thanks her friends from the bottom of her heart and begins thinking about which sweets to prepare for the coming session. A good sign, she hopes.

*

Usually, in moments of great unhappiness, the woman returns to writing.

It almost seems that the need to remember, to record what has been, only comes to her when she suffers, that suffering is the only time when the written word becomes a balm for her troubled heart. She isolates herself, listens to the silence and is thus able to feel deeply. And to penetrate into the recesses of her soul.

Happiness, those wonderful moments in which one says I'm Happy! when one smiles and would always like to dance, must be lived. She doesn't feel like sitting at the table in front of the computer, taking the time to reflect, to bring out the beauty that she has inside and translate it into written words. She does not have the time. She fears that the enchantment may vanish and so wants to enjoy it to the fullest.

And yet, when it happens, when it all ends, she regrets not having documented the joy, that rare sensation of being completely open, free and ready for adventure in the present moment.

She reflects on it as she thinks about all that has been lost following her separation from Albert, the return to solitude, missing his warm body in bed at night, the evening conversations on the phone when he was leaving for a reportage around Australia, the weekends spent together in the bush, endless walks, in the evening the dazzling fire with the hot soup, the magic of the starry sky without artificial light, the silence of human beings and the sound of leaves, of the animals all around. The inner music unleashed by love.

Now, at night, it's the dreams that keep her company.

Recurrent dreams that always have to do with the house, always different houses, rarely the ones she has lived in.

Her parents' house and in particular the terrace of their bedroom from which she soared happily into the sky, that was her constant dream in her adolescence. These, however, are absolutely unreal, fantastic houses, sometimes impossible houses, houses that she examines, criticises, admires, would like to fix, would like to live in; she likes them a lot or she walks away from them with a sure step. Houses in the city, near the sea, houses in the sea, in the bush, usually large and very complex houses. Sometimes deserted, sometimes full of people. She rarely sees Albert in any of them; often there is a man who then, for various and often absurd reasons, abandons her. In her dreams she felt it, from the beginning she already knew about the dramatic end, and there is a whole crescendo of unfulfilled expectations, always more, always more, a dramatic film which usually ends with a slammed door, a slap, a goodbye or a betrayal.

She now wakes up early in the morning.

In her half-sleep, she tries to go back to the sensations she felt, without thinking, without stopping to lick the wounds, she doesn't want to think about the day that's coming, she just wants to remain with the dream, whatever it may be, but with the dream. Naked and raw. Who knows if it might not be able to tell her something important, something that she cannot understand when she is awake. She takes up the pen and begins with the eyes half-closed almost as in a trance, to write spontaneously in a notebook of recycled paper with an emerald green cover.

She writes. Is this a beginning?

*

Late spring, living room on the ground floor, TV on, front door to the castle open.

A hot day, summer is getting close.

The first room one comes across upon entering Busby, immediately on the left, is the former bedroom, which has now become a beautiful sitting room. It is therefore now an important room, the room which, as soon as you enter, conveys the tone of the house.

Without the former small worn-out door but now with two large twin entrances cut into the thick sandstone wall, it lights up the corridor, finally, and immediately allows one to admire the beautiful lacy three-part window. A wall bookcase, facing the windows, holds all of Giacomo's philosophy books, those brought with him from Italy and those bought locally before his death, as well as other volumes acquired by her in the following years, and by her children more recently. On the left, the majestic armchair of nonna Vittoria, now restored, an antique armchair, made to be comfortable, in which the woman curls up in the evening to watch TV, often falling asleep in it. Facing the two entrances is a small Italian sofa, bought, as before, in Canberra from the same former fleeting lover. Between the two entrances and therefore in front of the sofa, is a brand-new television set.

On this hot day, numerous friends venture into the room; they arrive in different groups, go to the kitchen to fill their plates, into the corridor to chat, into the front garden to smoke a cigarette in the shade of the orange tree now in full bloom. They then return, worried, to look at the election results on the television, hastily explained by frenetic commentators, which make everyone ever more apprehensive.

Still fragile, her affair with Albert ever present, gripped by feelings of wrenching melancholy and of inconsolable loss, there are now times, however, when she begins to resonate with happy memories without regrets. She looks around. She likes the renovated Busby and, in spite of everything, is happy to be living upside down. But that part of her, the part that makes her feel at one with the greater community, that which holds that the *res pubblica* should be managed for the good of all, that part is profoundly dissatisfied. At this moment her rage returns, the rage that reddened her cheeks during her political activism in Italy, when in Rome she was battling for university reforms, for equal wage increases for everyone in the factories, for the great political changes that never took place. Her generation has paid dearly for having put itself on the line, for having fought for the common good. Many hopes, many mistakes, many failed attempts. A lost generation. Dispersed into a thousand rivulets, dismembered. And yet the desire for change has remained in many of them. She feels it when she returns to Italy and talks to her friends of the good times of long ago. A time that was also that of their youth.

At times she feels as though she is living on another planet. Since then many new things have happened, at least for her: in her personal life but also in her perception of politics and of what now are the important issues to fight for. Australia has given her a big jolt. In its alternation of governments, between Labor and Liberals, the country nevertheless still has a strong framework which is the bureaucracy (an unthinkable notion for an Italian!), independent of the parties and devoted to the common good. For this reason, despite the fairly regular political turnover, the country is holding up well, the economy goes ahead without hindrance and people trust the institutions. This, too, had been unthinkable for her.

What, however, leaves much to be desired, above all in the case of the right-wing governments, are the country's relationship with the Aboriginal population, and its foreign policy. These governments attempt to erase the shame of the invasion, never officially admitted, by senselessly spreading money around for "the improvement of the quality of life of the Aboriginal population" but the economic gap remains in place and gives no hint of diminishing. A recognition of the Australian First People has not yet made it into the Constitution, a Treaty between the invaders and the First People has not been stipulated and this

> (VOICES OFF)
> ... and that unfortunately this terrible right-wing government already in place for quite a while would not be disappearing with these new elections, that now the economy would be the prevailing religion; and that now they, the Italians of the recent generation, would have to think about finding themselves permanent employment: gone the casual jobs; gone the group houses, the squats, the dole! For the bureaucracy would now become more powerful and more complicated under this pettifogger Howard;

that who would have ever thought it when they had arrived in the early 1980s, fed up with the Italian swindles and the language of politicians who talked of parallel convergences, that now half of the population would approve of Howard and his acolytes, despite the nefariousness of the Tampa Affair which resulted in Christmas Island no longer being considered part of Australia in the case of the asylum seekers. And this, despite the lie about parents throwing children off boats to get asylum; crazy stuff! The government had excised parts of the map of Australia in order to prevent the landings of asylum seekers. This was the hard truth, that the human rights of refugees had been completely trampled on, that white racism was returning with Howard, who continued to be its champion. Disgusting that refugees would now be sent to Nauru, the tiny bankrupt island on the Equator which agreed to take care of them in exchange for rich Australian subsidies, when instead in the 1980s the boat people from Vietnam had been received in Australia with open arms. Moreover, that Howard now slavishly supported the post-September 11 policy of George W. Bush, and by adopting this hard-line approach had again won the elections. So now what would become of all the dreams of the Italian expatriates trying to make a new life in this new country where they had hoped to live happily ever after? And what could they do now if not huddle together in front of the television in that southern spring of 2001 with their eyes wide, their hearts in turmoil, but silently accept the anticipated victory of the Right? What could they do if not eat a plate of pasta, always delicious, always reassuring, but the political situation, damn it! was deteriorating at breakneck speed...

*

Uncultivated and abandoned for quite some time, then embellished with an orange tree which bears fruit twice a year, the front garden, following the renovations of the castle, also undergoes a marked surgical operation. In the hands of Maurice, a gardener friend who is also a poet and photographer, that rectangle of land often full of weeds, an interregnum between the street and the house, is transformed into a corner of the Appian Way, an Appian Way without the maritime pines, with two hedges of rosemary instead of laurel and with the crooked little path that leads to the entrance of the castle made from local gang sawn sandstone instead of the basalt stone used by the ancient Romans. An Australian-style Appian Way. That's how Maurice had described it to her when he had, with great enthusiasm, attempted to have her imagine and approve the project.

And now, with The Angel Wing, the sculpture in rusted iron which Amit has designed and some new Vulcan has bent while red-hot to his will in the workshop on Wonderland Street in Bondi, the castle also has its celestial protection. The Angel's wing is a very light but imposing screen, full of almost transparent curves, set slightly askew at the beginning of the little path so that the way to the front door is not in a direct line, again in order to cater for the feng shui preferences of some imaginary but potential future Chinese buyers.

At the centre of the garden the orange tree reigns supreme in front of the triple window. For the woman it represents the Tree of Life – the Australian version, of course – but it always reminds her of the magnificent one that she admired in the Cathedral of Otranto, that magical mosaic which fuses monotheism and polytheism, religious symbols and mythical emblems, astrology, the Breton cycle, fantastic animalistic figures, even an Alexander the Great ascending to the sky on two griffins. Of course this tree doesn't bear fruit twelve times a year as the Apocalypse would have it, but it is always full of deep green leaves and on hot days she is always happy to seek out the shelter of its shade. She feels protected. The scents of orange blossom and rosemary meld, the morning light illuminates everything and gives strength to the oranges that grow in profusion.

Curious neighbours are invited to pick some when they are ripe. One student makes jam with them, a female friend uses them for almond cakes; the woman prefers them in salads with olives and fennel.

*

The little apartment built in place of the laundry is the greatest innovation.

Partly excavated from the sandstone in a Herculean effort to prevent the seepage of water, it overlooks the three back gardens and is shaded by a very beautiful fern tree which has grown in only a few years (but, as we know, in Australia everything grows very quickly).

One large room with sliding glass doors, kitchenette, a generous bathroom. It's accessed from the little side alley, now refurbished, paved with old bricks. It's thus separated from the main house and it's for this reason, but also out of necessity, that the daughter settles in there after breaking up with her boyfriend with whom she's gone to the desert. Everyone is very sorry about the separation, especially the mother; the young man is the son of dear friends with whom they had been pleased to regard themselves as parents-in-law. For the woman, it had been a bit like finding a family that she did not have in Australia, but the tragic death of her daughter's father has left a deep mark on the girl and probably brought to light differences with her boyfriend that already existed and which in that situation became irreconcilable.

Losing her father, losing her boyfriend of five intense years, the daughter withdraws into herself. Again the mother finds herself in troubled waters, again she has difficulty navigating them. A distance has been created between them that seems insurmountable to her. The father is now the distance between them. His death has deprived his daughter of the possibility of a rapprochement, after many years of separation. On account of the mother and her irrepressible passions. Did she have to follow her lover, later to become her second husband, in his overseas postings? Did she have to remain abroad even when the main reason for doing so was no longer there? Didn't she think about her daughter, about her feelings, about the suffering of her separations? This is what the mother believes is stirring in the mind of the daughter who takes refuge in a worrying silence which the mother is unable to fill. She feels afraid to speak, to say the wrong thing that might reopen wounds and recriminations.

Regret for what she should have understood torments her. She therefore works hard to prepare appetizing dishes often left untouched by her daughter on the table in front of the glass door. She suggests books on meditation to her, invites her to go out with her, to meet friends, to go for walks. The daughter's silence towards the mother lasts a long time and the implied recriminations make themselves felt in the silence and in the few laboured conversations. The small apartment provides the daughter with a warm nest in which to finally overwinter the mourning.

The mother is pleased to have provided that, at least.

*

CBD late morning, city skyscrapers glittering under a spring sun.

For the woman, her daughter's return to Busby coincides with the return of her own imaginary shadows of her first and also her second husband.

Not that they had ever left but now they are present as figures in cinemascope. What comes to mind, one day when she is wandering aimlessly for a while and rather lost in the city, is a Woody Allen film in which his mother's giant face appears high in the New York sky as he is walking in a daze between the skyscrapers.

Why both husbands?

Death unites them, no matter how different, absolutely different they were, how different her love for them was. Death with which she had been forced to square accounts twice, with its trails of enormous suffering.

Since she was little she has always been afraid of dying. Or rather of getting sick from a terrible disease and then dying. It must certainly have been connected with her father's tuberculosis when he was young and from which he miraculously recovered. It had been whispered about behind closed doors and never in the presence of the children even though the three of them – they would tell each other later on – had sensed that there was a taboo in the house regarding their father's health. He always had to rest, had to be careful to never get cold and if he came down with a fever, it was a great worry for the whole family.

Over time, the woman had developed a desire to confront this fear. Consciously or unconsciously she fought it and won when she rebelled as an adolescent against the authoritarian and traditional wishes of her mother regarding her only daughter. Or when as a university student she dedicated herself, body and soul, to the revolution and felt that she could die happy on the barricades, red poncho and clenched fist.

Courage, which according to Chinese medicine, resides in the lungs, the organ that also collects the feelings of loss, mourning and therefore death, has the capacity to defeat fear, to annul it, to make it ridiculous and petty.

And then in Australia, the infinite horizons, the depth of the ocean, the bush stretching as far as the eye could see, the ancient wisdom of the indigenous people and the equanimity of Oriental practices, had offered her a new way of alleviating pain, of seeing the contrast between life and death in a different way. A dramatic opposition and, the more deeply one thought about it, an unreal one, because life and death are often imagined as two compact and separate entities, when in reality everything changes and transforms every thousandth of a second, even within us, even we ourselves change continuously. Dust we were and to dust will we return? As part of the great cycle we, wandering atoms, will mix with the leaves, the butterflies, the crabs, the crystals, the clouds of the sky. Gregory Bateson resonates within her with his poetic scientificity.

Why these thoughts right now?

Digressions, yes digressions that console, the woman realises as she looks indifferently at the shop windows, all lights and colours. It's digressions which, as usual, help her in such dark moments. Like this one.

She is unable to face the real difficulty of her relationship with her daughter, always much loved but often not understood in depth.

That's what she tells herself. Then, jolting herself from her torpor, she runs off to Central Station. She is going to be late. The driver of the 378 very kindly holds the doors open for her; luckily, she will arrive at Busby in time for the private lesson.

*

The daughter's return to Busby also brings about a new change in the fragile balance of the post-renovations period.

The actress reluctantly agrees to leave the studio apartment and will move in with friends at Bondi while waiting to find a small apartment all for herself.

A few tears, several cups of tea; she will maintain, she promises, her contact with the family.

The mother leaps into action. Also counselled by her female family friend who has an eye for decor, she begins to transfer from upstairs excess furniture and items which the daughter might like and which are missing from the austere luggage that has arrived from the Bronte Beach apartment she had been sharing with her boyfriend.

The brother hovers around, apparently indifferent, up and down the various floors of the castle. His sister is quite a bit older than he is, and perhaps he's feeling uneasy. He's aware that she is in pain but doesn't know what to say to her.

He is often on the street playing football with his friend Sean, right in front of the little lane that leads down to the studio apartment, so that he can keep an eye on what is happening. He follows everything but says little.

Dorian often goes down to visit the daughter with whom he has over the years maintained a very close and trusting relationship; the mother thinks that he was in love with her and perhaps still is. They will talk, she imagines, about yoga, meditation, art. Not of love, that is for the moment a no-go topic for the daughter.

A series of friends, especially very trusted female friends, take turns at her bedside when the girl feels very down and doesn't want to go out but stay home and do nothing.

After a while, which however seems an eternity for the mother, it becomes clear that a ray of light is opening up a space in her heart. She feels better or at least, shaking herself free from her inertia and paralysing negativism, she is beginning to take control of her life again. She goes out sometimes, finally! and with friends goes to the beach, goes for walks. She reconnects with disciplines that can help her recover: she returns to yoga, meditation and then begins to undergo therapy. Finally she manages to extract and deposit in the arms of an expert, the burden, too heavy for her young shoulders, which the death of her father had imposed on her. She begins to hope again.

She talks about traveling, starts making plans, consults with a friend with whom she does yoga.

She decides in the end to go to India, a country loved and regularly visited by her father due to his jewellery and antique business.

The mother rejoices in secret.

*

Wintry evening, living room lit only by nonna Vittoria's candelabra.

The preparations have been hectic:

- a snapper with a dead eye

- a realistic-looking gun

- a silver tray for the fish

- a laid table

- never-ending quantities of food

- unsettling music

- fake blood

- a number of photographic cameras

- a video camera on the tripod

- an old-time pot-bellied Italian grandfather

- a good-looking young man with a mafioso moustache

- a ditzy waitress.

The final exams of the dreaded HSC are approaching and the son who has never worked hard in his school career is now really committing himself to the only subject that truly stirs his passion. He has organised, and is now shooting, a short film in black and white on the theme of the Italian mafia in Australia.

He has co-opted the family of his friend Antony, his father who is a tiler, his retired grandfather and, indeed, Antony or Antonio, a handsome boy who will follow in his father's footsteps and will enter into partnership with his parent after finishing high school.

The mother is pleased; she knows that her son has a keen eye and that the many films they have seen together have provided him with a rich cinematic culture. His inspiration, it seems to his mother, is a mixture of the use of extreme wide-angle shots à la *The Trial* of Orson Welles, in which the low ceilings of the Palazzaccio in Rome had created a claustrophobic atmosphere, and the gangster films of Martin Scorsese. She doesn't say anything in order not to irritate him, and she doesn't offer any advice, even if she would like to. She can see that he is very anxious; he has little time and he left it to the last minute, as is the Italian style, while in Australia planning ahead is a must. Wearing a short apron over a black dress as the typical waitress, the woman places the fish on the tray and prepares to enter the scene. It's a very short scene: the fish is the symbol of a betrayal which must be paid for with death. Around the table the protagonists exchange their last words in strangled voices, then a shot and the tray fills with blood. Nonna Vittoria's candelabra projects sinister and canted shadows on the ceiling and on the wall behind the table.

In the end, at the very end, the son has picked himself up: he has begun to study, he has salvaged everything he could after years of lack of interest and exclusive dedication to the god of soccer. He has even begun to be a little interested in the subjects he has to study.

The mother breathes a sigh of relief. Her anxiety, her worries about this boy without a father now seem unwarranted; a bad dream from which she has finally woken. She feels that a weight has been lifted from her shoulders. She relaxes and has fun following the unfolding of this intricate film noir from the wings.

*

The new staircase now allows the corridor to get a lot of light.

Designed by Amit and custom-built by a very talented Iranian artisan, a master craftsman with serious expertise in measuring spaces and choosing wood, the space in between each step reveals the entrance to the living room, then the light blue terrace and beyond it, the sparkling sea. The railing is made of metal cables supporting a light wooden handrail. Open at both front and back, the staircase is a light sculpture in the middle of the corridor, each step opening onto a different view, different even according to the time of day and therefore of the light, each time prompting differing reflections.

The woman sits there one morning at dawn to read and reread the letter that her daughter, who has been travelling overseas for a few months, has sent her from India, the first stop on an intensive yoga retreat in Rishikesh during the *Kumbh Mehla*.

Finally, after a period locked into her suffering, the girl has managed to pull herself out of her desolation. She has decided to pursue her interest in yoga more deeply with some good teachers. She would like to specialise in it and then begin to teach it.

The letter has greatly moved the mother; she will conserve it forever. It seems to her that an opening may have been created and that, from a distance, the mutual affection that has always been there, overshadowed in recent times by heavy tragedy, is beginning to shine through again.

In a sweet way, the daughter describes the retreat she is on with a dear female friend of hers; she writes enthusiastically of India, of the ashram where she feels at ease, in harmony with the world around her. She'll be staying there for another month and a half. She's made the right decision, thinks the mother. Travelling, not as mere escape but as a way of going deeper into things, seems to be bearing its fruit. An acceptance of the inevitable, of what has already tragically happened, is a long process whose stages also depend on how we are and how we are used to dealing with events, the mother knows it well. She also knows that in her young life her daughter has already faced many difficult trials – her celiac disease, her parents' separation, moving away from Italy, adapting to different countries – so she hopes that she will be able to work through, in meditative silence, the loss of her father. The letter is a good start, a beautiful gift for the mother who presses it to her heart.

The pinkish light creates a rainbow on the wall of the corridor; she now likes this corridor which had given her so many problems before the renovations. Finally.

*

A series of the daughter's friends have been staying by turn in the tiny studio apartment, formerly the laundry, since the girl decided to start traveling. Some pay rent, others come for only a few days and the mother is happy to host them. Some are very meticulous and leave everything in order, others instead leave a mess. Sometimes the mother lets it pass, sometimes she doesn't.

The daily management of the restructured Busby comes to weigh on the woman's mind. Between the children, the tenants, the university, her private lessons and the many other interests she is trying to pursue, she always has little time to occupy herself with everyday matters: putting on the washing machine, dusting, washing the floors, cleaning bathrooms and kitchens. Above all, she has no desire to do it. She has never really done it. Forever, in her life, there has always been a woman to come and do the cleaning. In the family home, in the houses she has had with her husbands, in Rome or abroad, there has always been someone else, always a woman, women with often troubled lives, often wise and resourceful women, women whom she found interesting, women to whom she was very attached as a child and then as an adolescent; the housemaids have been the ones who have always taken care of her basic needs.

How crazy is that! She wanted to carry out a revolution, she wanted to change the world, solve humanity's problems but she has always had someone else to wash her sheets!

She doesn't really know how to keep the newly-renovated castle in good condition, how to thoroughly clean it, really thoroughly. Where should she begin?

Even during the period of Giacomo's illness, when the Australian welfare system did its utmost in a thousand ways to help her by offering babysitting for the child, shopping, cooked lunches, a car to take her to the hospital, etc. etc. the only thing she had accepted enthusiastically was the cleaning of the house. That she had just been unable to do. Above all the floors!

And yet, she's now reading Thich Nhat Hanh's poems on how to meditate while doing household chores and being able to rejoice whilst doing it. After all, isn't the house, the care of the house, a metaphor for the care of the inside of oneself? So, that's exactly her problem. The outside as a loophole. She searches for a compromise.

Through friends, twice a week she employs Norma, a Chilean woman, a single mother with two dependent children. She will clean bathrooms, kitchens and yes even the notorious floors. But the woman herself will cook the meals in the evenings while reciting:

Present Moment

Wonderful Moment

*

In addition to the interior, Busby now also requires maintenance on the exterior.

It seems that when you start doing work on one part you then have to restructure all the rest. Indeed, just like in life when, one is aiming to reach a new equilibrium after the previous balance has been broken.

The new part at the back of the castle, all three floors painted in a colour matching the sandstone of the old part, being exposed to the winds and the lashing rain that at times come from the south, requires constant touch ups.

Even the fixtures of the windows and of the unvarnished mahogany glass doors must be oiled regularly, and the balustrades of the terraces lose their colour if they are not periodically restored to the famous tropical light blue.

That's how it is. One needs a handyman. If you don't want, in a couple of years, to see the exterior of the castle, that is, the rear part, prematurely age. The old part, being made of stone, will live forever but the rest, made of highly perishable modern materials, must be looked after continuously.

With her bank statements at hand, the woman understands that she couldn't afford to hire the services of even one other person, but she has no alternatives.

The choice falls on the friend of a worker who has carried out the long and painful renovations. The worker is Greek, the friend is Russian; noisy and hasty. One never knows when he can come to do the work. He continually cancels appointments, then swoops in without warning when perhaps no one is home and improvises what needs to be done. Sometimes he hits the mark and sometimes he doesn't, often omitting something important, as for example a water leak from the terrace on the third floor which has penetrated into the living room ceiling. A real disaster; for two weeks a bucket to catch the inexorable dripping proudly occupies the centre stage in front of the white sofa in the living room.

The woman sometimes thinks that she should look for an alternative to the Russian, but she doesn't have the time or desire to dedicate herself to it and, in any case, the Russian is nice and cheerful, and the children like him. So she muddles on.

But that's not the end of it.

What about the front and back gardens? Will they look after themselves? The lawn at the front, the orange tree, the rosemary hedge, the beautiful plants in the gardens at the back? In a short time and given the subtropical climate, they will soon morph into a jungle. Here, too, further expenses!

On the advice of a female friend, a local gardener, a young and smiling Lebanese this time, will take care of cutting the grass every two weeks and pruning back luxuriant trees and bushes when necessary. The gardener is meticulous; he does exactly what was asked of him and is very reliable.

His fees, however are quite high.

And so, the costs of the renovated Busby continue to visibly increase. The mortgage will need to be extended.

*

As usual, when worries increase, the woman distracts herself with a new engrossing adventure.

This time she accepts an assignment from FILEF, a left-wing Italian association that also operates in Australia, to coordinate an ecological project that is very close to her heart and which is about food: it involves the promotion among Sydney's Italian Australians, especially the generation that immigrated in the 1960s, of organic products threatened by the arrival on the market of GMOs.

She will be paid for it, not much but she will be paid, and this is the excuse she gives herself for taking on yet another commitment.

Ever since her daughter was one year old and had developed celiac disease, the mother had been forced to closely examine all the food products she bought to see whether, hidden behind the usual eye-catching and misleading advertising, they contained gluten. Thus the list of ingredients on the packaging was the only thing she read very carefully and she has acquired considerable experience in the field.

As soon as the agreement with FILEF has been concluded, the woman throws herself into the project with enthusiasm. She gets in touch with Australian ecological associations, with anti-GMF groups, with the Greens; members of FILEF are part of her action group.

The living room at Busby fills up little by little but ever more chaotically with leaflets, posters, signs, press releases for local radios, and activists always proposing new action plans. Talking points are prepared for meetings and debates. The topic is new and draws the curiosity of Italian Sydneysiders, mostly living in Leichhardt, Five Dock, or Haberfield. The public meetings are a great experience for the woman who often, at the end of meetings, hears people recount incredible life stories to her. Often about hardship but also of achievements.

It is decided that the ecological campaign should conclude with a major event: presentations by experts and live music from the Wind from the South, a musical group made up of recent expats, will accompany an organic dinner prepared by the Italian Vice-Consul, who's an expert chef.

Great food, great music, very persuasive proposals regarding future activities.

A great feeling of satisfaction for everyone. Or so one hopes.

The printed material for the project is then carefully culled; part of it is preserved in the FILEF archives, part of it distributed among the activists, and part of it is recycled.

The woman can finally regain possession of her living room and lie down blissfully on the very comfortable white sofa without being overwhelmed by tons of printed paper. Silence returns; one can again notice the scent of honeysuckle, the ocean in the distance, the fern tree springing up from the garden. Order reigns supreme at Busby. At least for the moment.

*

After India and a brief return to Sydney, the daughter flies to Europe; Italy, of course, but also Switzerland and England. She is engaging ever more intensely in yoga and meditation courses; they are doing her good and she is following particular traditions. The mother realises that she is becoming interested in monastic life. It could be her life in the future, the daughter seems to be trying to say to the mother when she phones to share her news. The mother becomes agitated and, after many sleepless nights, she decides to speak to her openly at the next phone call.

The young woman has just turned thirty, celebrated with a great party at her uncles' house, with its wonderful terrace overlooking St. Peter's, and her dear cousins all showering her with love. Italy fascinates her and she begins to miss it, especially when she has to return to Australia. In a long, long international phone call, she talks to her mother about her family in Rome, her friends and, as her mother had foreseen, also about the Buddhist monastery in England where she has stayed as a lay guest, engaging in Buddhist meditation with the most interesting teachers the West can offer. She would like to spend an extended period there and then... who knows ...?

The anxious mother interrupts her and gives her a brief speech prepared during sleepless nights. She never knows if what she is saying is the right thing but in this case she feels in her deepest being the need to face up to what is a crucial issue in a woman's life: motherhood. So she tells the daughter point blank but with a slightly racing heart that she can become a Buddhist nun at any age but that's not the case with having children. She is thirty now and must try to understand, to avoid regretting it later, if she feels the desire for motherhood.

Silence at the other end of the phone; the mother understands that she has, perhaps, hit the mark. The daughter thinks about it and doesn't answer. Silence. The mother changes the subject.

They'll discuss it further at a later time, the mother hopes to herself.

*

The son's room, one morning.

In medio stat virtus (Virtue lies in the middle) declared Horace in one of the schoolbooks at the Lucrezio Caro High School.

The middle room on the top floor, now illuminated by a second window, becomes during the day, when her son is at school and she doesn't go to the university, the room for her reflections, the room for writing.

There, right under the window on the right from where, stretching one's neck over the sandstone walls, one can see a strip of ocean, is situated the only computer in the house: the brand-new, beautifully designed Bondi Blue iMac.

There the woman feels protected and focused. She steps over the monumental mess left by her son: the corpses of his discarded clothes, the piled up and neglected books, his minuscule Star Wars Indian-ink drawings, his countless tee-shirts and football boots, and sits down at the computer.

It's there that she has begun, after so many years, to write poetry again. She has already found a title that she really likes: "Austranaut".

It will be made up of memories and emotions, present and past, Australia and Italy commingling, learning to live together within her. At least, so she hopes. After years of lacerations, of exhausting conflicts, of never definitive choices (Sydney/Rome, Rome/Sydney ?), she now feels calmer. She is staying in Sydney, for the moment. Now she lives in the restored castle, the children have by this stage grown, her job is casual but always renewed annually. Now she is more accepting of her condition as a woman wavering between two languages and two cultures; some losses, some gains. She looks around and she recognises herself in the people she sees on the street; she seems to comprehend the suffering but also the richness that she reads in the eyes of others and their complex histories.

*

In-between lessons, one afternoon, the mother receives an unexpected phone call from her daughter. Pleasantries, conversation about life in London, Australian expatriate female friends she has rediscovered. And what about future plans, her mother asks. Here a little hesitation.

Then the bombshell: in a monastery in Sussex the daughter has met Nolan, a former Buddhist monk whom she really likes and with whom she has recently become involved. She is convinced that her mother will like him too. She is returning to Australia in a few weeks and he will follow her shortly after.

Something has unblocked in the daughter's heart.

The pain at the loss of her father which was preventing her from opening herself to life, which required continuous physical and spiritual discipline to avoid giving herself up to despair, seems to have lessened. The passage of time loosens tensions, dissolves them. The cycle of life that repeats itself day after day – the woman has experienced it – creates a progressive distance from the original pain so that it can be observed without one feeling swallowed up by it.

A new life.

The woman begins to imagine a thousand possible future scenarios, all different from each other, all positive, all with the same Mills and Boone ending. She asks herself what kind of young man might this be, to have captured her daughter's heart? She begins to clean up the little apartment, she wants to make it beautiful, to render it welcoming.

Always the same hopeless romantic she says to herself, a bit of self-irony fortunately not lacking while with a big brush and soapy water she erases the footprints of the last careless guests from the floor of the apartment.

*

In the back garden there is now, on the third level that borders on the garages, among the wild plants which are growing out of all proportion, a fairly large space, artfully paved with bricks by Maurice, the gardener-friend. There now, in the centre, there's a beautiful pond with papyri, lotus flowers and red goldfish. There also are two deckchairs in which to rest in the shade on burning hot days. It's there that the woman withdraws for a moment when she wants to relax and escape the continuous movement that seems to her at times to agitate the castle. The son joins her one still-cool morning; he sits next to her, a few minutes of silence, the mother understands that he wants to talk to her.

Having just returned from a long period in Italy, the son confesses to her that he has decided not to immediately enrol in the university, as his mother would like him to, following the family tradition. He will also now abandon his dream of becoming a champion soccer player, something he has passionately wanted for many years, and instead will devote himself to a project that excites him at the moment. He wants to create an event management company.

The mother looks at him in a sidelong glance. He has just turned 18, celebrated with an unforgettable party. The mother organised it for him against his will even if in the end he had been very happy with it and had thanked her for it. It had been huge and had featured live music performed by a gypsy accordionist that the mother had by chance heard busking one day in the pedestrian area of Bondi Junction. He had played Italian, French and Spanish songs, all dance tunes, all arousing nostalgia in the woman and the expatriates present. And then, after the cake and candles, the son's friends had taken him to a pub where alcohol had featured prominently in the traditional initiatory ritual into adulthood of young Australian males.

He will create the management event company with his friend Jason, his all-time best friend since they had first met at the International Grammar School. Together with him the son has navigated his high school years, concentrating very little on what he needed to study and a great deal instead on the recreational activities which the school offered: a professional basketball court on the roof with a view of the city, camps, end of year parties, Sport, especially his much venerated soccer. With him he would spend his weekends and holidays, between the beach, outings with friends, rushing back to Busby or to Jason's place in order to dress up for the evening. All the time, endless discussions regarding what they should wear in order to attract the girls at private parties or in the bars which they tried to crash even when they hadn't reached the legal age of 18. In Jason, the son had found an older brother, only slightly but older, but a brother who could in part make up for the loss of his beloved father, remembered only through the mother's stories of him, as he had been only two and a half years old when his father had died. It was a loss the son had tried to fill with photos, memorabilia, fountain pens, watches which the father collected, but above all by maintaining a close relationship with Gino and Robbie, old friends of his father who had thus become his adopted uncles.

The mother looks at the son in silence. She is speechless. She didn't expect such a rapid and radical change of plans. The idea of a business venture causes her dismay; it isn't a family tradition, she doesn't understand anything about administration and accounting, and she cannot imagine how her son, who has just graduated from high school, can possibly get his head around organising a business about which, until now, he has been completely in the dark and which will completely change his daily habits. No more waking up at dawn and hurrying to soccer training, no more careful dieting and abstaining from alcohol, but instead up until 3 or 4 in the morning, sleeping during the day, contacting hundreds of people with invitations, shows, music and marketing for each event. His business will be called "Pony" and on the business card already prepared and which her son shows her with pride, there is a beautiful galloping colt. He and Jason have already set up a work plan and initiated a lot of contacts. It will all go well, you'll see, mum, she seems to hear him saying with his captivating smile. Still unable to speak, the mother rocks in her deck chair, feeling the son's enthusiasm and desire for approval. When she finally speaks, she endeavours to be positive and to accept the inevitable.

*

Again a change.

In the eyes of passers-by, and for the neighbours and friends who often visit, Busby is always a surprise. Every time a different film.

This time it's the daughter's return. Trips, experiences, encounters through which she has matured a great deal – everyone notices it, everyone comments on it when they compliment her as they toast her return.

Once again the tenants have disappeared from the studio apartment, again the furniture has been brought down from the floors above, again the daughter's friends, male and female, begin to reappear. Once more the mother is preparing pasta dishes for everyone, upstairs and downstairs.

And that's not the end of it. All are awaiting curiously, with growing interest on the part of everyone and a little anxiety on the mother's part, the arrival of the daughter's new boyfriend. Through often-interrupted conversations that are also many times resumed, the mother forges some idea of this relationship which, for the girl, is positive and reassuring. Born in an environment familiar to both of them, the monastery of Amaravati, apparently one of the most renowned in Europe for the teaching of Theravada Buddhist meditation, developed through the communal practice and shared spiritual intentions and life, the relationship appears to have solid foundations.

Their plans are many. They will travel through Australia, then maybe return to Europe, perhaps to England. The daughter now has the sparkling eyes, the easy laugh and the deep voice of when she is happy.

The son, as is his wont, appears all of a sudden, and then disappears; he comes out of his room and makes himself a huge bowl of Weetabix, listens for a short while – there's always something new to hear – caresses the cats that are his passion, his children, his brothers; the wise Cosmo is, at times, also his father. Then he'll disappear, reappearing all dressed up. His friends arrive and he disappears again. It's obvious that he's happy at his sister's return.

Dorian decides to go and live in Bondi and rent a separate studio as his jewellery workshop.

The mother once again takes possession of the large bedroom on the first floor.

*

Nolan's arrival from England brings great excitement to the castle.

Finally the daughter, in multicoloured Indian clothes, and with curly hair cascading onto her shoulders giving her the appearance of emerging from a Renaissance painting, has brightened up. She's in love. She often goes from the studio apartment to the floor above, chats with her brother and mother, recounts her adventures in India, in Europe. They're amusing adventures, at times alarming; adventures she's had on her own, with friends, sometimes with Nolan, a young Englishman with a lovely smile, reserved but attentive to everyone and everything. The girl has many ideas, many projects in mind and looks for her boyfriend's approval; it's clear that being together with him allows her to dare. Her joy, after so much suffering, has a general beneficial effect on everyone.

At last the mother feels that Busby is the castle of a Happy Family.

From her vantage point of the large bedroom upstairs – furniture changed again, nonna Vittoria's dresser, the George V table, the bed with the single backrest, all brought back up and put back where they had once been – the woman sees what is happening around her in a mixture of reality and imagination.

As in the Hollywood films of the 1950s, the lawn is sparkling green, the recently-renovated castle is perfect. Romantic music (is it perhaps Doris Day singing?) spills out into the street. The front door opens time and again, and the inhabitants repeatedly dance in and out, all joyful and content.

Above, below, front and back, there are no longer any dark corners or black holes. The light penetrates everywhere, the many windows bring the outside inside: the ocean, the trees, the scent of honeysuckle first and foremost.

There is a sense of fulfillment, or at least this is what the woman feels when she hears the cheerful chatter coming from her son's bedroom, the smell of the vegetable soup that the daughter, helped by her boyfriend, is preparing for them all in the large kitchen, the sound of bowls being distributed to visiting friends amidst a lot of shouting.

Is it love that is having this effect?

The young couple spend a great deal of time in the studio apartment, then go out, walk along the cliff, meet a few friends; often eat with the mother and son, then return to the studio apartment perhaps to meditate again. They exude a sense of peace and quiet, a novelty at Busby. They decide to stay in Sydney for a month or so, and then to go to the Blue Mountains to work in a Buddhist Theravada meditation centre in Medlow Bath, 1,000 metres above sea level, crystal clear air and thick bush as far as the eye can see. The plan to go back to Europe seems far away.

The mother relaxes, finally.

*

It is late at night.

The door of her room opens softly. The woman opens her eyes and Nolan, stock-still at the front of her bed, whispers to her that the daughter has gone into labour. The couple will remain in the small apartment downstairs for as long as possible and then they'll go to the hospital. He lets her understand that they would prefer to manage the event alone. They will call her when the baby has been born.

The return of her daughter to Sydney, the subsequent arrival of Nolan, their departure several months later for the Blue Mountains, the daughter's unexpected pregnancy and the couple's decision to thus return to Sydney, all in quick succession, have been such major events and have followed each other in such a rapid succession that the woman has not yet been able to digest their import. She is engulfed by a happy bewilderment.

And now the birth of her little granddaughter, so powerfully moving. Immediately a lump rises in her throat. She remembers her own pregnancies, knowing that this is a delicate moment in which anything can happen; each childbirth is its own event with an always unpredictable course. She is worried for her daughter. The woman is unable to sleep. She gets up and wanders around the castle several times, trying to relieve the anxiety while straining to hear whether everything is ok.

Towards dawn, having just gone back up to her room, exhausted and sleepless, she sees the car moving off; the thought of the hospital at that point reassures her.

She remembers the birth of her daughter in Rome in a private clinic assisted by a gynaecologist whom, at the time, she trusted unconditionally but whom later, during her feminist phase, she would criticise as having "too American" an approach.

Her waters had broken but she wasn't dilating fast enough so he had given her an injection and presto! in a few hours the little girl had been born and with a slightly swollen head due to the aspiration that the doctor had deemed necessary. But the baby was so beautiful! The mother had been very young and very happy; childbirth had been an extraordinary experience that she then remembered with joy, unleashing the incredulity and almost the ire of many of the feminists in her consciousness-raising group. They, at the time, were focused on the issue of abortion, which was the mantra of the moment, certainly not on births, considered painful and often imposed experiences to be avoided as much as possible. For her, on the other hand, it had been what she dared to call a cosmic experience; in the past she might have called it a miracle. One that becomes two; surely that's something extraordinary?

Her son, on the other hand, had been born in Sydney at the Royal Women's Hospital in Paddington although, then too, after a whole day when her waters had broken but she hadn't dilated enough. And so hours of waiting and miles of walking along roads, streets and lanes, so much so that in the end she and Giacomo had quarrelled. But then at the hospital, everything had gone smoothly and they were in love and in agreement as never before. The child, too, little thing that he was, so dark, ever so dark, with a blue-black spot at the base of his spine. Had he perhaps been bruised during the birth? Reassured by the Indian nurse that darker-skinned children have a concentration of pigment which then spreads all over the skin, the woman immersed herself in a happiness without bounds.

So happy at that point, with two children, a girl and a boy, two relationships, two different experiences, what more could she want?

And now at the dawn of her granddaughter's first day of life, she is preparing to become a grandmother.

When she was small, she had not had her grandparents close by; three had already died when she was born and the last grandfather, Angelo, lived in Ortona and she rarely saw him. She has always missed her grandparents: an older and wiser presence than that of her parents, a special and unconditional affection.

So, now, she wants to be a good grandmother. She is 57, with lots of positive energy and a great desire to give everything she hasn't had.

She washes, gets dressed, watches the sun rising over the sea and settles down to wait for the call from the hospital.

*

Hot evening, terrace of the bedroom on the first floor.

The birth of her granddaughter has meant not only for herself, but also for her daughter, a revisitation of the past.

The 1970s in Italy, with communal life, group management of children's lives, and the dream of revolution at the centre of life, contrast sharply with the attitude of the new generation. Now more aware of the importance of the first years of life, parents are totally dedicated to their children in those crucial years, even at the cost of considerable sacrifices in their personal life.

The woman reflects on the first therapy session she has attended with her daughter a few hours earlier. It's very painful for her. Having to acknowledge that she had not given enough consideration to her daughter when she was young, that she hadn't thought about the consequences of her impulsive decisions, it has been difficult, even embarrassing. Her political activism, which had brought with it the dubious distinction of sampling some of Italy's prisons, the separation from her husband and her period of experimentation with free love at first, then travelling the world together with her new lover, dragging her daughter with them, the choice to stay abroad even after everything seemed to be over – Giacomo had gone forever and the great dream of the end of the rainbow had vanished in the short three months of his fatal illness – all this now takes her back to the unresolved tangles of her childhood when she took refuge in dreaming with open eyes in order to avoid the reality which she perhaps couldn't understand. Dreams which subsequently had always to do with falling in love, with feeling loved, finally.

It was thus that the constant factor of her life had always been her relationships with men, one after another, and if they weren't there, she felt at a loss. An emptiness within herself.

The death of Giacomo, the father of her son, had delivered her a colossal blow. Not only the loss, but the loneliness as well. She has had to learn to be alone. She has had to; she had no other choice.

It has done her good to have had to apologise to her daughter. She has lifted the lid on a boiling pot. Now everything that has accumulated in there can come out and she can look at it. She will continue. After the therapy sessions with her daughter, she will continue with her own individual therapy. Still in time.

*

In the car, at two in the afternoon, heading towards Busby Parade.

As soon as the session is over, the woman, at the helm of her white Toyota Yaris, summarises for herself, as if in a dream, the results of the 50 minutes spent with the therapist.

Fifty minutes all to herself, away from the crowd of friends, from the homework of students to correct, the bills to pay, the shopping, the children, even the cats. Fifty minutes which she thinks are well worth the half hour of traffic from Bronte to Neutral Bay across the Harbour Bridge overlooking the Opera House (always stupendous) and the two extra lessons that she had willingly taken on in order to pay the fees of Jana, the German psychologist/psychotherapist.

She has decided; she wants to come to terms with herself, finally.

Thus, the weekly stories which, in the early meetings, she recited in an often mechanical manner, as if they were the chapters of someone else's life and had no relation to her, under the attentive gaze of Jana, which misses not a thing, not even the woman's position when sitting in the armchair or on the couch, nor the rhythm of her breathing or the changing tone of her voice as she narrates this or that, are now coming to be transformed into intense moments of the past, relived in the present. The tears that suddenly flow, the longings, the regrets, the wonderful memories and the painful recollections, all accumulate without any apparent sense, but they do all come from her soul.

And it's there that she needs to go in order to comprehend herself, to understand the reason for those dark and uncontrollable moments that make her feel alone and without a firm point of reference. It's not the culture or the ideologies, the political stances or the work choices that frighten her. She slips her way through those without any problem; all that comes easy to her, almost naturally. Her father stands there in the background reassuring her with his open mind, his unlimited knowledge and his great affection.

Her mother, on the other hand, has always been a problem for her.

"I breastfed you until you were almost two years old", she used to tell her when the mood took her.

The greedy and passionate relationship with the breast, the warmth and the smell of the maternal body, the closeness of the parents' bed at night, all this then abruptly interrupted when she was almost two years old by the birth of her little brother.

"He's premature and frail, we've placed him in the crib next to us with lots of swaddling around him to keep him warm".

So busy with her little brother, her mother had no time for the little girl who was chubby and full of health. And her reaction? She had been deposed! Her little wooden bed with its horizontal bars, which she leaned out of as soon as she woke up and smilingly embraced the world, which was, of course, her mother near her, had been abruptly transferred one night – she will remember it forever -, into the room of her bachelor uncle. Without explanations, without a single word that she at least may have understood. And during the day?

"We've hired Marisa, a girl from Tagliacozzo who loves you so much".

Marisa had held her in her arms, made her white, fragrant meringues, and would take her out to the Quirinale Gardens, not far from the house. She was the substitute. But the maternal warmth, the laughter that resonated inside the little girl when her mother allowed her to jump on the bed, the shared intimacy, the space and time to grow while being watched over step by step, none of this had been any longer possible. Or perhaps the mother hadn't considered it necessary because she herself hadn't received it from the stern and daunting nonna Vittoria. She too had been placed second to her brother, the bachelor uncle into whose room the wooden bed with the horizontal bars had been moved.

"As a child you were always serious, very serious. Your brother on the other hand was always smiling".

So the mother as a little girl had been without words, lacking *les mots pour le dire*, as Marie Cardinal would have put it. Without words to explain herself, to ask for things, to throw the well-known tantrums, without being able to cry and then laugh complicitly with her mother, the little girl, imprisoned in her silence, had developed an inner world made up of diversions, dreams and romantic fairy tales. In effect, she had had to mother herself.

"Act like a young lady and not like a tomboy! Go and make your brothers' beds".

It is certainly from there, from her relationship with her mother that all her difficulties have emanated, the emptiness that she sometimes still feels, the fear of abandonment, the existential insecurity, the rebelliousness. The woman now understands this more and more while Jana listens to her without speaking.

She has always known all this. Perhaps in a confused way and without ever engaging in serious in-depth analysis or being able to form a precise picture, a picture that might have reassured her, that might have told her to look with love on that little girl with chubby cheeks and the pensive look, that ever critical teenager. It's from that pain, that original painful lack, that her rebellious attitude was born, her need to be loved and her desire to do something important, to leave a mark.

Along with an understanding of her own past, little by little, there in Jana's study, with its warm-coloured walls and soothing aspect, the woman also comes to realize the possibility of a better understanding of her mother, always loved in spite of everything, even if in a complex and visceral way, the possibility of imagining and seeing her in the social and cultural context in which she had grown up, without a father and with a very authoritarian mother, and consequently of understanding the choices that she had made, consciously or unconsciously, for her daughter.

Not only. In session after session, the images return: small faded photos in black and white of a beach, perhaps Anzio, perhaps in summer, and her mother as a little girl hanging on, together with her brother, to the skirt of nonna Vittoria, all in black.

A young widow with two young children, suddenly without money, like her; like her, having to let out the rooms of her large and beautiful apartment.

A cycle which repeats itself.

Her grandmother, her mother, herself and now her daughter.

A chain of strong-willed women, each one with the difficulties that life has presented to them, each one who has tried to face and resolve those difficulties as best they could.

This is the legacy that her daughter has received and that she will have to deal with and reflect upon; the mother hopes that her daughter will be able to draw from it the strength and ability to transform it into wisdom for her future life.

*

Son's bedroom, late October. Spring in bloom.

Having returned to Sydney after a wonderful holiday in Italy on the Dolomites with her younger brother, her sister-in-law and some friends, the woman decides to begin writing her autobiography. Another family tradition, as she suddenly remembers.

Her story, she thinks with growing enthusiasm, given the variety of what has happened to her, the countries where she has lived, the experiences she has had, could be of interest to her family, but not only to them. She has a degree in Sociology and she has always been interested in the dynamics of human behaviour and social phenomena, so she thinks she may be, objectively, an interesting case study. However, she does not want to stop at the level of content, at the mechanical enumeration of important events of her life. It should be an autobiography that might encapsulate the bare hard facts but should also follow the development of her thinking and her transformation over the years.

She begins to trace the memory of the most salient events. She feels happy, it's a good exercise for the memory. Along the way, she hopes, the recollections will gradually become more precise, and with them the emotions that accompanied them. The therapy she is continuing to undertake with great interest will help her, she is sure. She realises that she must find a guiding thread that will unify the narrative. Not an easy task.

One morning, spontaneously, she finds a good way to begin:

Today I am sitting at the computer because I have understood; I write these words because I have shed the blood.

The scars are deep and always remind me that happiness is a decision.

And now I have decided.

The form in which the story will develop takes up a lot of her attention.

She has in mind an old love of hers, Gertrude Stein, and her writings which reflect the fluctuating movement of unpolished thought, often repetitive, a form of stream of consciousness much adopted in the consciousness-raising feminist groups of the old days. And then she also thinks of the infinite labyrinthine paragraphs of Marcel Proust and certainly, most recently, those of K.O. Knausgaard or the vulnerable but fearless memoirs of Annie Ernaux. A style, then, that might permit her to write spontaneously, something that works well for her when she feels inspired and doesn't pause to analyse too deeply. She remembers that over the years she has collected, in a grey and white fabric folder now quite worn-out, all the writings that she's been happily conserving, the best that has come out of her soul. She fetches the folder and rereads the jumble of handwritten, typed or computer-printed sheets.

She realises that she really quite likes some of the pieces left in the portfolio and forgotten for many years. Perhaps they could be included in the autobiography which, after a while, is taking on the lineaments of a memoir or the Anthology of a Life, a collection of medium-length narratives that all have to do with her life. After all, what else could she write about in this ever more intertwined, interconnected, entangled world that has, at this point, joined into one? Whereas once upon a time a writer would have been locked away in her village, her province, her country, and would have thus been eager to overcome the insurmountable limits of geographical knowledge through the imagination, she is now exposed to winds coming from everywhere, to the most detailed, most extravagant, most horrifying information, where reality itself far exceeds the imagination.

"Rome Sydney Round Trip" could be the title. With the passing of time, the woman becomes ever more passionate about the idea of putting together a sort of mosaic, a puzzle penned at different times, places and styles.

Discontinuity has been, after all, the characteristic of her life; first a great passion which initially generates movement but eventually dissipates, like a meteor, before regenerating in a completely different way. There's no common thread there, the woman says to herself, but isn't the passing of the years the only real common thread? Why become fixated on finding one? Isn't deep down everyone's soul complex, twisted, made up of attempts, steps back and forth, darkness and illuminations that alternate over time?

*

Busby is at its best:
> Front door open
>
> lit candles in the garden

lights in all the rooms

flowers at the entrance

live music

and lots and lots of people.

Ten years have passed since the woman returned to Sydney and today she turns sixty. Incredible.

In the living room on the long glass table, food in abundance, good wines, a colossal dessert; her son and her daughter have spared no expense and even make two fine speeches. The mother is moved.

She has put on well-worn jeans with a tight black T-shirt. Her one indulgence is a pair of French two-tone cream and blue stilettos, bought used at Vinnies for $15 but beautiful, and, of course the three-stranded pearl necklace around her neck, a gift from her mother. She is happy. The evening unfolds between a lasagna, a chat, live music and reunions with new and old friends dug up from past address books. A swirl of emotions, loud peals of laughter; she could not have asked for more.

Later, in the small hours of the already looming morning, in bed under the duvet, the woman asks herself how she feels at sixty.

These ten years in Sydney, following her return from Canberra, what have they been for her? She has done so many things: university teaching, one year of educational radio broadcasting, conferences in Australia, conferences in Italy, a member of the Italians Abroad

Committee. And yet this is all doing, as they say here. And what, instead, about being?

Lots of meditation and lots of yoga; the woman knows they are good for her but she can't manage to do them alone, she always needs a teacher to spur her on.

Her children have been for her a difficult knot to unravel. Has she been a good mother? She has great doubts. And for the rest? Deep inside, how does she feel inside?

Life alone with two children on another continent has forced her to mature, no doubt. Above all, thanks to the children with their requests, their criticisms and their expectations.

But other questions pile up in her slightly tired mind.

The indelible question always returns: why did she leave Italy, accompanied immediately afterwards by: why has she remained in Australia?

She left, undoubtedly, due to a desire for adventure, certainly in order to forget the political defeat of the Movement.

But also to detach herself from her family where, even if nurtured with respect and affection, she felt bogged down, always disappearing into other people's lives which she judged more important and more interesting than her own. She hadn't been able to be herself, to like herself for being who she was. At times there was a darkness inside her but she never gave herself enough time to shine light on it.

For this reason the spaces, the enormous sun-drenched spaces of Australia had so fascinated her upon arrival, perhaps because they reflected the yearnings in her soul for the possibility of receiving light.

Spaces that also required an extended time to be traversed and thus, a time allowing one to understand, to grow, to mature.

Thinking about it more deeply, the Australian desert has been the most important discovery of her stay in Australia.

As soon as she had landed in Alice Springs the first time with Giacomo, she had felt that this was a place where she could live forever. Was it the air, was it the colours, the sand, the rocks, the people or everything together? The energy definitely; that land imbued her with a strong energy mixed with deep emotions, a sort of poetic inspiration that she had hardly ever felt before. And which had been necessary for her to get in touch with her most remote essence. She had felt happy. They had travelled continuously for three weeks, walked, swum in pools of chilly water under a blazing sun, climbed primordial rocks. They had loved each other there as never before. She had felt she was on the moon, in a place possible only in the imagination and therefore fantastic. She continually wanted to sing; her voice gushed from deep within her and resounded in her heart. She was sure it was there that their son had been conceived, there had begun a very happy period in her life. Three years, no more. But three years lived with joy in the heart and a smile on their lips.

And so when Giacomo had suddenly died, a precipitous fall had been inevitable and she had realised that the ground was missing under her feet. Unprepared, totally.

Now, at sixty, what does she say to herself on this night of her birthday, under the warm duvet where no one else can hear her?

She likes herself, at least a little, now. She understands that she did what she could with whatever knowledge, sensitivity and experience she had at the time. She has come a long way.

After all, she has learned, yes, she has learned this: that there is no precise point of arrival.

And that the path is the goal.

*

Summer evening, lounge room opening on the terrace.

Sparkling wine in abundance, a quick cold supper; a multitude of friends have gathered to toast the victory of Kevin Rudd, the new Labor Prime Minister. Later there will be more celebrations, in the streets, in pubs, in clubs, all night long. A lot of enthusiasm, a lot of positive chatter. The woman is also happy because her son has finally acquiesced to go out with her and her friends, roam the streets to hear what people are saying, gauging the lie of the land, making sure it's true then, that it isn't a dream: the government has changed and Howard has been defeated. For once her son goes out with her, this handsome and imposing young man, thick, dark mane, strong energy, overflowing with ambition. Now a member of Greenpeace, he often criticises his mother, an environmentalist *ante litteram*, whom he judges as too moderate. He is in a phase of extreme fundamentalism, sparked from having seen *The Inconvenient Truth* by Al Gore, a flash of inspiration like that of St. Paul on the road to Damascus. And the decision to completely change his life. Enough of Pony, the business he has created with his best friend, Jason, with night-time events at Kings Cross, music, alcohol, girls, designer shirts and trousers. From now on a frugal life, intense activism, weekly meetings at Erskineville with his local Greenpeace guru, training in the Blue Mountains, long hair, second-hand clothes, vegetarian food, many personal reflections recorded in his large notebooks. He talks about going on a motorcycle trip to Africa with Jason, using his ecological inspiration to make a positive contribution to the indigent people of Africa. Before departing, however, he wants to dedicate himself to promoting environmentalism among young Australians of his generation. He is very happy with Rudd's political platform and for this reason has decided to go and celebrate in the city with his mother.

    (VOICES OFF)

    ... that finally something was changing, that Kevin 07 finally represented some hope! That after 11 very long years of the Howard government, caught up in their own private concerns, engulfed by the financial woes lamented night after night by Treasurer Peter Costello on TV; that finally a light could be seen piercing the darkness, that issues close to the heart of the many expatriates returned to the foreground because Kevin Rudd was promising to sign the Kyoto Protocol, the 60% reduction of CO_2 emissions before 2050, the dismantling of offshore detention centres for asylum seekers, a computer for each student in the last four years of secondary school, billions for new social housing and health equality for the Aboriginal people, as well as – of utmost importance – official apologies for having removed them as children from their families of origin and forced them into assimilation with white invaders; that finally there was talk of politics again, of a vision for the future, a future for everyone, not only those with money; that they, the Italians who had arrived Down Under in the 1980s could now breathe a sigh of relief because all was not lost and they could begin to think again that they had done well to move to the other side of the world, that it hadn't been a mistake, as they had often feared during the dark Howard years, that one could go back to thinking about getting involved in politics as in the past, not exactly like then but that, in any case, there was again a place in society, in Parliament and in the media, for issues such as the environment, multiculturalism, justice for disadvantaged social groups, that there was, after all, still hope...

*

Late morning, front garden.

The son has prepared, under the soon-to-blossom orange tree, a brunch for his mother who has just returned from the desert.

Ten days of meditation in the MacDonnell Ranges: a swag under the stars, waking up at dawn, ten hours of silence each day, everyone motionless, sitting cross-legged on the dried-out bed of an ancient river. All exposed to the winds raging without mercy, or to the scorching sun that makes everything sparkle in winter in the central desert.

The transition back to life in the city after a period of group solitude, after having moved away from everything that is habitual in order to reach the essential and be able to look deeply inside, is not easy, and the son seems aware of it. He leaves her sitting under the scented orange tree and goes to the kitchen to make scrambled eggs. The woman is happy to be able to remain silent a little longer; she looks around and feels with all her being the colours, the sounds, the smells, known, but now magnified and foreign. On the desert plain she had gradually distanced herself in memory from familiar elements; she had reached a moment, on the sixth day, when she felt equally distant from her past departure and her future return. A moment when she was there in that deserted plain, ringed by hills full of glittering stones that seemed to speak to her, a moment when past and future no longer had any importance, any depth, a moment when she had stretched out on the ground, had felt totally present to herself, had felt herself breathing in harmony with the Earth.

Very busy with his business, only a few months old – it's called *Adverto* and this time dealing with websites, videos, photos, and documentaries – the son is happy and hopes to put aside enough money to soon leave. He has, nevertheless, found time in his busy day to go pick up his mother at the airport and spend a few hours with her. She is grateful to him for it.

The son returns from the kitchen with slightly-burnt eggs, but for the mother they are special and so she thanks him, fills her plate, chews slowly and then little by little begins to speak. She tries to tell him something about the experience she has been through. She notices he's attentive, but she can only provide hints. She doesn't even know how to recount – one can't recount, one can only experience it – and this is what she tells her son who, intrigued, promises her that he'll go to the Blue Mountains with Ale, his best friend from Canberra, to do at least a weekend of meditation before leaving on his trip to Africa.

*

Sun-drenched afternoon, kitchen, around the marble table.

The daughter and her partner approach the mother who is preparing dinner.

Always glued to the shoulders or the chest of one of them is the little girl, brown curls like her mother, a real darling. Very calm, cautious in her choices and movements but adamant when she makes up her mind;

her grandmother adores her. She often looks after her now but when she was first born, she was a miracle that the parents wanted to enjoy in private; they had to get to know her and make themselves known. After the first three months the grandmother came onto the scene. Always worried about doing the right thing, little by little she manages to find a regular routine that the toddler really likes. Twice a week in Busby's large living room, the woman puts on an Argentine tango, always the same one, gathers her granddaughter in her arms and starts dancing. And then both of them on the ground, on the large Persian carpet bought in Canberra together with her dearest friend, Patricia, rolling and unrolling coloured ribbons, jangling together the four aluminium bracelets from Lamu, that island so close to her grandmother's heart. Her son is a bit jealous of this enormous attention paid to the little girl. For 18 years he has been the youngest of the house and now he feels dispossessed, but he is too old to acknowledge this feeling and, a little frustrated every now and then, he bursts out with some recrimination always directed towards his mother.

In the absence of their fathers, the two children have only their mother on whom to vent their discontent. And they do it often, the woman says to herself when she remains calm and does not get furious.

Now she looks at her daughter and her daughter's partner with serene eyes.

Ever since their move to nearby Birriga Road, they are both more relaxed.

The option of living in the larger area of Busby has, unfortunately, not worked out. For some time the young family had occupied the upstairs middle room and the room with the terrace, the former pink room, while the mother had been staying in the large bedroom and the son had been in the small studio apartment in the back garden. This arrangement, however, had not lasted long.

Stairs, terraces, the one bathroom on the ground floor, many open spaces and very few doors, shared utilities, booming voices downstairs that could be heard above, the mother's life without regular hours, the front door always open at all hours, the brother with his noisy friends: all this made life difficult for the young couple living their first experience with a very young child. The mother would have liked to please them; and she tried, but without success. So they found a 1930s apartment in a quiet area, ten minutes walk from Bondi Beach, fifteen minutes drive from Busby. It shouldn't be but, even if she hides it and superficially accepts it, their moving out has been painful for the mother who sees it as a personal defeat. She knows that it's normal for children to go their own way when they've become adults but she would have liked to have them there, well and happy, at renovated Busby, for a bit longer, so as to counteract in her memory the darkness of the past years. A dream. In any case, they often come to visit her and she always cooks special dishes for them. They are vegetarian and, between Italian and Japanese macrobiotic cuisines, the mother always manages to discover appetising recipes. They are finding a new balance. The son likes visiting them at Birriga Road; it's a novelty for him who, at this time, is always on the run and hoping to soon leave for his trip to Africa.

Today the daughter and her family have arrived early for dinner. They've had a brilliant idea they say, and seem very excited.

After some hesitation, the voices overlap and in the end, the unthinkable, the inconceivable.

Why not sell Busby now?

Now?! Yes now!

The market is good; they have done some initial research. Being renovated, the castle should be worth quite a lot and with the proceeds they could buy three small apartments: one for the mother, one for the son and one for the young family.

The woman, shocked, doesn't reply. This proposal is a kind of blow to the heart and she doesn't know what to say.

From the kitchen, through the two openings that give out onto the living room and from there to the glass doors, the view is expansive, beautiful. She looks at the sea. It's calm, an intense blue, typical in winter.

The idea is totally unexpected, the woman feels unprepared.

After two years of turmoil, demolition, reconstruction, refurbishment, reorganisation, for a year or so now Busby has been looking magnificent; it's a pleasure for her to live there. To open her eyes every day and remember that it's over, that she has made it – it's been tough but she has made it – is a new feeling of lightness. There's only the mortgage that worries her because, unfortunately, it's increased a lot.

Flustered, she says she will think about it and that they will talk about it again at dinner, with the son also present; now she must finish cooking.

Between the sautéed vegetables and the azuki bean soup, the woman begins to order her thoughts somewhat, a whirl of ideas that always come back to the starting point: sell Busby?!?

It's pure folly, a backward step. Busby is their story in Australia, it's the cornerstone, the anchor they've clung to in the darkest moments, the point of reference to which one can always return. Even before the renovation, as ruined as it was, it emanated a warm energy, everyone was attracted to it.

Completely out of the question.

And yet, and yet…. she has always trusted her daughter who has always made wise decisions. Why does she now think it's better to sell?

As the hours go by, with the daughter, her partner and the little girl gone for a walk by the sea and the silence in the kitchen broken only by the odd afternoon bird passing by, the woman reviews the renovations for the first time with a different eye. With a critical eye.

With regret, she suddenly realises that she has concentrated above all on aesthetics and has not thought about the practical side; she hasn't thought about the near future, that is when her children, now grown, would need their independence. She wanted, after so much suffering, to make Busby a jewel. She had wanted to realise the dream she had had with Giacomo of a large renovated house in which to live this new overseas life with their children, who were small at the time. All together.

Can the daughter be right? Do they need three separate spaces? Perhaps living all together is the dream of the mother, not of the children?

And then an illumination, a worrying insight that she should have had in the past and that now lives only in the impossible time of the hypothetical, of the if-only-she-had-thought-about-it-before.

She should have made the castle into three apartments! A very small one for herself in the attic, the mini apartment that already exists in the back garden for her son, and a larger apartment with bathroom and kitchenette for her daughter and family on the first floor. In addition, a kitchen, bathroom, living room and lounge on the ground floor for common use. A colossal blunder. They could all have lived there together, that would have been their home and their story, but all three of them would have had their own independent space. The daughter would not have moved out and the son might not have been leaving. Perhaps.

And she? She's now alone in the big, renovated castle.

She has spent a lot of money, taken out a big mortgage to pay for the work and after all that, she could never manage to start all over again.

Too late! Very upset. And the vegetables are almost burnt. A little Mozart to lift the spirits and dinner is finally ready.

Around the Frate table, with a sea breeze that feels almost lukewarm after the sun-filled day, mother, children and son-in-law try to make sense of the many proposals, questions, answers that bounce around, the voices that get louder, things unspoken but felt in the air, regrets for what could have been if instead ... She looks at her children with a tenderness mixed with dread. She feels that she should talk to them with an open heart, make them feel at ease in expressing their own emotions about their history, about Busby and its sale. She understands only when they get to the dessert that she should be the one to pull it all together. As always, she gets a lump in her throat when she has to dig up the past. She has always been the woman of the future, of new visions, the past has never been important to her and now more than ever she wants to forget. But not her children, her children are young and want to reconstruct their history; Italy, Australia, they want to know and talk about how things happened, in order to build a life on solid foundations, not on quicksand, even if, as the woman uneasily notes to herself, perhaps it's no coincidence that they've lived precisely in a castle made of sand.

Long silences after so much enthusiasm and fast talking. It will take time to digest this possible unexpected change; the woman isn't up to making a decision at the moment. She'll think about it she says; calmly, she'll think about it.

And she leaves everything, as often happens with her, in abeyance.

*

Time passes, everything is still suspended.

She has to make a decision but she can't do it; it's too painful, too many memories, too many risks. Too many doubts.

As soon as she can, the woman goes for walks along the cliff.

Bronte-Bondi or Bronte-Coogee? Seven km. the first, almost 8.5 km the second.

Walking is good for her; especially at the fast pace that gives rhythm to her thoughts, it helps her to unravel her mental tangles. In difficult moments she can't sit still, she has to move, her body has to get tired, it needs to feel at the centre in order to allow her turbulent mind to catch its breath.

Nature is her ancestral mother. She turns to her when she feels lost, when there are important decisions to make.

She has very precise memories of

- running at breakneck speed along the Lungotevere Flaminio in Rome with Laika, the very beautiful family dog, when her young boyfriend, Andrea, fellow high school student and her first great love, wanted to leave her for someone else and she didn't have the courage to confront him

- pensive strolls under the burning Sicilian sun, up and down up and down between the prickly pears and orange trees, uncertain whether to telephone or announce in person to her parents when she returned to Rome that her path would now be inexorably marked more by thoughts of revolution than of religion

- escaping from the tent and the campsite in Crotone one full moon evening to reach the ruined castle where her political leader was waiting for her to make love and ask her to flee to Canada with him

- walking barefoot on the beach below the family home in Anzio, undecided whether to accept marrying Silvio and living a "regular" life or dedicating herself totally to political activism

- wandering aimlessly around New York Central Park while waiting to hear from the lawyer if she could return to Italy or would have to remain there illegally with her little girl for an indefinite time

- disturbing visits immediately after Giacomo's death to the Gap, in Watsons Bay, Sydney, overhanging the ocean and famous for suicides

- evening excursions to the Bronte cliffs gripped by Hamlet-like doubts: to return to Italy and the bosom of the family or accept the job at the Australian National University in Canberra?

- refreshing swim at Tuross Head, decisive in her decision to abandon

Canberra and return to Sydney.

The woman sets off.

Bronte-Coogee is the longest route and that's why she chooses it. Maybe she will have more time to make a decision.

On the cliff overhanging the sea, she re-examines what possibilities lie before her: stay in Busby and find other work that allows her to pay the increasingly large mortgage? Or sell, and with the proceeds hope to buy three small apartments, for the daughter, for the son and for herself?

The thought of leaving Busby tears her apart. It's the story of her family in Australia, her history with Giacomo, the story of a journey shared with many expatriates, friends and acquaintances. It cannot be erased.

However, a future including being lonely in the large three-storied mansion frightens her somewhat; she doesn't want to let out rooms and finding other work to pay the mortgage doesn't suit her. Teaching requires time and energy and added to what she's already doing, would mean doing it all badly. And, then, should it come to her needing it, in Australia she doesn't have the support of her family and can't lean on anyone. Alone with two children in a foreign land: it seems like a nineteenth-century serialised novel.

At times, exasperated by the twofold possibilities (always two! Something to do with her being a Gemini?) she decides to choose one at random and stay with that for a while, to see how it feels. The one that stays with her the longest, that will be the one to choose. Right or wrong, only time will tell.

*

Late spring, 11 in the morning, a large sign in the front garden advertising the sale of Busby at auction.

Well in advance, in a pinstripe suit, exuding a slightly sharp perfume and a dazzling smile, the auctioneer arrives and with a certain assurance chooses the best place in the lounge room to set up the table to hammer out the sale. Right in front of the large glass doors with a view of the sea.

Busby is a work of art.

In addition to the structural renovations which are still brand new and the furnishings which, at the direction of the estate agent – a tall, slim young woman looking like an Australian model or a Hollywood star –, have been renewed, Busby's ambiance has now been enhanced by

- a beautiful Aboriginal painting that casts marine colours in the corridor

- red goldfish in the glass vase in the living room to ward off the bad luck of past times

- colourful Indian pillows on the sofas

- a Nigerian mask in the kitchen above the round marble table

- a Kenyan xylophone in the bedroom, formerly the pink room

- a little skirt, hand-dyed by the women of the island of Kiriwina, hung between the two windows of the large bedroom right above nonna Vittoria's George V coffee table

- and then: plants, flowers, vases, bowls full of fruit, grouped together more according to colours than flavours

all these complete the stage set.

The owners want to sell at this point, at all costs.

So much indecision, dancing back and forth, second thoughts, discussions, consultations; the woman has finally understood, has accepted and thrown herself into the enterprise. So she hopes. She's unable to be still for a moment; as soon as she's made the decision, she doesn't want to rethink it, she doesn't want to doubt again, she wants to act, act, act. She wants, most of all, to convince herself that this is the right solution.

It will no longer be Busby, it will be something different, but it will certainly be a new life without the traces and the nostalgic memories that, inevitably, the castle at times brings back to her. Above all without the loneliness that would undoubtedly await her in the big mansion, now that her daughter lives elsewhere and her son is about to leave for Africa.

At 12 o'clock, the fateful hour, prospective buyers begin to arrive, curious passers-by, neighbours, supportive friends (there will be a bite to eat once the sale has taken place).

The auctioneer works hard, with a captivating voice and an eagle eye to ensnare possible buyers.

Hopes are high, feelings are palpable.

But no.

After so many preparations, the house doesn't sell for the amount that mother and children had agreed would be enough to guarantee a comfortable future for all three. Above all, the absence of a bathroom in the upper part of the house is a serious handicap according to many possible buyers, mostly wealthy young people infatuated with the idea of an en suite for each bedroom.

A bitter disappointment.

The real estate agent, having paid and seen off the auctioneer, approaches the mother and children with a reassuring look. She is sure that Busby will sell even if a little under the price they had envisioned. A few of the people who have come to the auction have left their business cards with her, saying they were interested in buying.

The family is also heartened by the friends: the toast is proposed in any case, the finger-food also arrives, the smiles return, the sale still seems at least possible, perhaps even imminent.

One still hopes.

EPILOGUE

Final night at Busby, large bedroom upstairs, a lit candle, sleeping bag

After everything, absolutely everything has been taken away

    in the big truck of the removalists

    in the little van of the second-hand merchant

    in her and her friends' cars

    in the large boxes of those who bought what the family no longer wants

After the municipal bins have been filled with wood paper glass plastic metal

    all to be recycled

    all in some way a part of the history of the castle

After her children, friends and workmen have left

    the odd tear, many hugs and a flurry of emotions

    with the electricity and gas disconnected, only the water left

After *les jeux sont fait* the woman decides to sleep for the last time, and this time on her own, at Busby.

She who has always been afraid to be alone in the house at night and who has chosen to sell Busby, in addition to many other important reasons, because she knew she would be the only one to remain in the great sand castle, this night, the last, she would like to sleep in it in order to savour its energy, to be able in the future to recall its smell of primeval stone.

The large bedroom is the room where she spent tragic moments with the terminally-ill Giacomo in the king size futon that he liked so much. It's also the room which, repainted, purified with incense, flowers and candles, then inhabited by various people in succession and finally by her for several years and now tonight for the last time, has given her much joy. She really likes this room; in the end, she does really like it very much. And yet she has decided to give it away.

Why is it that every time things are settled and when she could finally enjoy the peaceful flow of her life, something happens that obliges her to change, to commit herself, to throw herself into a new enterprise? Is it the difficulty she has to stand still, to consolidate what has already been achieved, to make herself stronger, to accept that, even if what she has is not perfect, it is certainly "good enough"? Is it her karma?

And yet no, this time it is not completely true.

She is leaving Busby because she has completed what she had started with Giacomo and what she had promised herself, and him, to finish.

She leaves Busby, above all, because she feels inside herself that finally she can leave it, finally she has fulfilled the dream they had as a couple.

Now she must learn to dream alone.

She doesn't know what will happen in the future, where she will go, how she will cope with this next change.

A reed in the wind.

After all, as Pema Chodron writes, "The truth is that we cannot avoid uncertainty. We must accept that we will never be able to know what will happen to us in the near future. This not knowing is part of the adventure of life".

She lies down on her sleeping bag.

The night is calm, all-enveloping.

Through the windows seeps a glow which she hopes is the moon. Yes, it's a sliver of moon high in the sky. And the stars, how many stars!

The Songlines....

She goes out like a light.

Farewell Busby, castle of millennial sand on the hill facing the sea, beacon in the fog of our hearts, life-saving anchor for drifting seafarers like ourselves.

You gave us solace when, outside, bitter tears were raining; you taught us to await the sun's return, you showed us the path to hope and cheer, of time that recalls all and comprehends all.

For us you made yourself more lovely, for us you opened yourself and now shine bright.

We go with light hearts, strengthened by the life we have lived in your generous womb.

We have grown, we have understood that life is a journey full of pauses, but still a journey, and that now it is time to begin again. After 18 years under your protection, Busby farewell!

VITTORIA PASQUINI

Born in Rome, 1946, political activist, feminist, academic and traveller, wrote *The Legend of Busby* while dreaming at Bronte, on land of the ancient Gadigal people of the Eora nation, who have always been and always will be custodians of the Sydney coast.

GINO MOLITERNO

Currently an Honorary Staff member of the School of Literature, Languages and Linguistics at the Australian National University, Gino Moliterno developed a strong parallel interest in translation while teaching courses in both Italian literature and Film Studies at the ANU. His first major foray into Italian-to-English translation was a stage-actable version of Giordano Bruno's sixteenth-century comedy, *Candelaio* (Candlebearer, Dovehouse Editions, 2000). After English renditions of all the Italian entries of Valerio Daniel De Simoni's *Diari/Diaries: Real Love for the Turning World* (VDSA, 2012) and De Simoni's later *Diari di viaggio/Travel Journals* (Luca Sossella, 2014), he is currently working on a translation of his own father's account of his immigration to Australia in the 1950s.